THE ONE WAY

for 11 - 14s

BOOK 5

CHRISTIAN FOCUS PUBLICATIONS

We believe that the Bible is God's word to mankind, and that it contains everything we need to know in order to be reconciled with God and live in a way that is pleasing to him. Therefore, we believe it is vital to teach young teens accurately from the Bible, being careful to teach each passage's true meaning in an appropriate way for the age group, rather than selecting a 'teen's message' from a Biblical passage.

© TⁿT Ministries
29 Buxton Gardens, Acton, London, W3 9LE
Tel: +44 (0)20 8992 0450 Fax: +44 (0)20 8896 1847
e-mail: sales@tntministries.org.uk

Published in 2003 by Christian Focus Publications Ltd.
Geanies House, Fearn, Tain, Ross-shire, IV20 1TW
Tel: +44 (0)1862 871 011 Fax: +44 (0)1862 871 699
e-mail: **info@christianfocus.com**
www.christianfocus.com

Cover design by Profile Design

This book and others in the series can be purchased from your local Christian bookshop. Alternatively you can write to TⁿT Ministries direct or place your order with the publisher.

ISBN: 1-85792-708-7

TⁿT Ministries (which stands for Teaching and Training Ministries) was launched in February 1993 by Christians from a broad variety of denominational backgrounds who were concerned that teaching the Bible to children be taken seriously. The leaders were in charge of the Sunday School of 50 teachers at St Helen's Bishopsgate, an evangelical church in the City of London, for 13 years, during which time a range of Biblical teaching materials was developed. TⁿT Ministries also runs training days for Sunday School teachers.

CONTENTS

On the Way for 11-14s / Book 5

Contributors:

Preparation of Bible material:
Annie Gemmill

Editing:
David Jackman

Activities:
Thalia Blundell
Jennefer Lord
Nick Margesson
Annie Gemmill

On The Way for 11-14s works on a 3 year syllabus consisting of 6 books. It builds on the 9-11s syllabus and introduces young teens to study the Bible in a way which is challenging and intellectually stretching. Because they are often unprepared to take things at face value and are encouraged to question everything, it is important to satisfy the mind while touching the heart. Therefore, some of the lessons are designed to introduce the idea of further Bible study skills, e.g. the use of a concordance, a character study, studying a single verse or a passage.

Lessons are grouped in series, each of which is introduced by a series overview stating the aims of the series, the lesson aim for each week, and an appropriate memory verse. Every lesson, in addition to an aim, has study notes to enable the teacher to understand the Bible passage, a suggestion to focus attention on the study to follow, a 'Question Section' and an activity for the group to do. The Question Section consists of 2-3 questions designed to help in discussing the application of the Bible passage. The course can be joined at any time during its 3 year cycle.

To prepare a Bible lesson properly takes at least one evening (2-3 hours). It is helpful to read the Bible passage several days before teaching it to allow time to mull over what it is saying.

When preparing a lesson the following steps should be taken -

1. PRAY!

In a busy world this is very easy to forget. We are unable to understand God's word without his help and we need to remind ourselves of that fact before we start.

2. READ THE BIBLE PASSAGE

This should be done **before** reading the lesson manual. Our resource is the Bible, not what someone says about it. The Bible study notes in the lesson manual are a commentary on the passage to help you understand it.

3. LOOK AT THE LESSON AIM

This should reflect the main teaching of the passage. Plan how that can be packaged appropriately for the age group you teach.

4. TEACHING THE BIBLE PASSAGE

This should take place in the context of simple Bible study. Do ensure that the children use the same version of the Bible. Prior to the lesson decide how the passage will be read, (e.g. one verse at a time), and who should do the reading. Is the passage short enough to read the whole of it or should some parts be paraphrased by the teacher? Work through the passage, deciding which points should be raised. Design simple questions to bring out the main teaching of the passage. The first questions should elicit the facts and should be designed so that they cannot be answered by a simple 'no' or 'yes'. If a group member reads out a Bible verse as the answer, praise him/her and then ask him/her to put it in his/her own words. Once the facts have been established go on to application questions, encouraging the group to think through how the teaching can be applied to their lives. The 'Question Section' is designed to help you when it comes to discussing the application of the Bible passage.

5. VISUAL AIDS

Pictures are very rarely required for this age group. A Bible Timeline is useful so that the young people can see where the Bible passage they are studying comes in the big picture of God's revelation to his people. You can find one at the back of this book. A map is helpful to demonstrate distances, etc. A flip chart or similar is handy to summarise the lesson.

6. ACTIVITIES AND PUZZLES

These are designed to reinforce the Bible teaching and very little prior preparation (if any) is required by the teacher.

- Encourages the leaders to study the Bible for themselves.

- Teaches young people Bible-study skills.

- Everything you need is in the one book, so there is no need to buy activity books.

- Undated materials allow you to use the lessons to fit your situation without wasting materials.

- Once you have the entire syllabus, there is no need to repurchase.

On The Way for 11-14s is designed to teach young teens how to read and understand a passage of Scripture and then apply it to their lives (see How to Prepare a Lesson). Before learning how to study the Bible they need to know what it is and how to find their way around it.

The Bible

Christians believe that the Bible is God's word and contains all we need to know in order to live in relationship with God and with each other. It is the way God has chosen to reveal himself to mankind; it not only records historical facts but also interprets those facts. It is not a scientific text book.

What does the Bible consist of?

The Bible is God's story. It is divided into 2 sections - the Old and New Testaments. 'Testament' means 'covenant' or 'promise'.

The Old Testament contains 39 books covering the period from creation to about 400 years before the birth of Jesus. It records God's mighty acts of creation, judgment and mercy as well as their interpretation through the words of the prophets.

The New Testament is made up of 27 books containing details of the life, death and resurrection of Jesus, the spread of the gospel in the early Church, Christian doctrine and the final judgment.

Who wrote the Bible?

The books of the Bible were written by many different people, some known and others not. Christians believe that all these authors were inspired by God (2 Peter 1:20-21, 2 Timothy 3:16). As a result we can trust what it says.

How can we find our way around it?

Each book in the Bible is divided into chapters, each one of which contains a number of verses. When the Books were written originally the chapter and verse divisions were absent. These have been added to enable the readers to find their way around. When written down they are recorded in the following way, Genesis 5:1-10. This tells us to look up the book of Genesis, chapter 5, verses 1 to 10.

At the front of the Bible is a contents page, listing the books in the order in which they come in the Bible. It is perfectly acceptable to look up the index to see which page to turn to.

Aids to teach the Bible passage

* Many of the lessons have activity pages that help to bring out the main teaching of the Bible passage.
* Packs of maps and charts can be purchased from Christian book shops.
* A Bible Time Line is useful to reinforce the chronology of the Bible (Timeline Pages 81-87).

Questions to aid in understanding

Periodically use the following questions to help the young people understand the passage:

* Who wrote it?
* To whom was it written?
* When was it written?
* What situation is being described? (if applicable)

THE BIBLE LIBRARY

To make a chart of the Bible Library enlarge the template below and photocopy as required. Draw 2 sets of shelves on a large piece of paper (see diagram). Label the shelves. Cut off the unwanted books from each set and write the names of the books on the spines. Glue the books onto the appropriate shelves in the order in which they appear in the Bible.

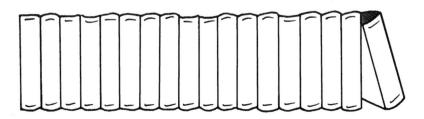

The Bible Library

Old Testament	New Testament
Law (5 books)	Gospels & Acts (5)
History (12 books)	Paul's Epistles (13)
Poetry & Wisdom (5)	Other Epistles (8)
Prophets (17 books)	Prophecy (1 book)

OVERVIEW
God's Plan

Week 14 | **The Judges**   *Joshua 13:1-7; 21:43-45; 23:1 - 24:33, Judges 1 - 2*
To understand that the difficulties Israel faced in the promised land were a result of disobedience.

Week 15 | **Call for a King**   *1 Samuel 8:1-22; 15:1-35, Deuteronomy 17:14-20*
To learn what kind of king God wants for his people

Week 16 | **David, God's King**   *1 Samuel 16 - 19, 2 Samuel 7*
To understand that David is God's chosen king through whom God's promise will be fulfilled.

Week 17 | **King Solomon**   *1 Kings 2:2-5; 3:1-28; 4:20-34; 8:1 - 11:25*
To understand that Solomon, despite his wisdom, was not the one who would bring rest for God's people.

Week 18 | **From Division of the Kingdom to Exile**   *1 Kings 11:26-40; 12:26-33; 15:1 - 16:34, 2 Kings 17; 24 - 25*
To show that God judged his disobedient people in the way he had promised.

Week 19 | **Prophets and Promises**   *see lesson notes*
To understand how the prophets fit into God's plan.

Week 20 | **Exile and Return**   *Ezra 1 - 3; 6:13 - 7:10, Nehemiah 9 - 10; 13*
To understand that return from exile did not bring the promised restoration.

Week 21 | **Review of the Old Testament**
To understand God's plan portrayed in the Old Testament and how this looks forward to New Testament events.

Week 22 | **Who is Jesus?**   *Matthew 1:1 - 4:25*
To see that Jesus is the one promised in the Old Testament.

Week 23 | **Why Did Jesus Come?**   *Matthew 4 - 5; 8 - 9; 16:13 - 17:13; 20:17-28*
To understand what Jesus came to do.

Week 24 | **Death and Resurrection**   *Matthew 21:1-17; 23:1-39; 26 - 28*
To see the significance of these events in the light of the Old Testament.

Week 25 | **The Spread of the Gospel** *Acts 1:1-11; 2:1-41; 7:54 - 8:8; 9:1 - 10:48; 13:4 - 18:23*
To understand the power of the gospel and its cost to the messenger.

Week 26 | **Judgment and Restoration**   *Revelation 20:11 - 22:6, Matthew 24:36-44*
To understand how finally everything will be restored.

SERIES AIMS

1. To understand the Bible's main story line.

2. To increase our appreciation of what God is like. As we see God reveal himself through his relationship with his chosen people, his character comes into increasingly sharp focus.

3. To give context to and confidence in Bible study through understanding the history and big themes of the Bible.

4. To understand how we fit into God's great plan.

MEMORY WORK

Weeks 1-5:

The books of the Bible in order.

Weeks 6-12:

But you are a chosen people, a royal priesthood, a holy nation, a people belonging to God, that you may declare the praises of him who called you out of darkness into his wonderful light.

1 Peter 2:9

Weeks 13-17:

We all, like sheep, have gone astray, each of us has turned to his own way; and the LORD has laid on him the iniquity of us all.

Isaiah 53:6

Weeks 18-21:

'I will put my law in their minds and write it on their hearts. I will be their God, and they will be my people.'

Jeremiah 31:33

Weeks 22-26:

Now the dwelling of God is with men, and he will live with them. They will be his people, and God himself will be with them and be their God.

Revelation 21:3

God's Plan

The usual way we study the Bible is by taking small sections of books or narrative and studying them in depth. This is of great value and is the main way we learn about God through his word. Very often time is short and, though we refer to the context of a passage, we do not have time to study it more fully. This can leave children (and adults too) with only a sketchy idea of the order of Biblical events and how they fit together.

This series is an opportunity to stand back from the detail and look at the whole story of the Bible. We aim to not only make the chronology of the important events clear, but also help the young people to see through these events the unfolding plan of God. For many the individual stories will be very familiar and they are ready for the challenge of fitting them together to see the Bible's 'Big Picture'. There seems to be a disproportionate number of lessons on the early chapters of the Bible, because these chapters lay the foundations on which the rest of God's revelation is built. Many well known stories are omitted or only referred to in passing as we focus on the Bible's 'landmark' events.

It is likely that large sections of this material will be new to teachers as well as to group members. Therefore the lesson notes have been written with the teacher in mind. We do not suggest that all the material in the lesson notes is presented to the group. Rather, that the teacher, equipped by the lesson notes, will be able to teach the material at an appropriate level for their group. The lesson plans suggest a way in which to tackle the material, covering the main points, and they assume a group time of at least 45 minutes.

PREPARATION

Genesis 1:1 - 2:7

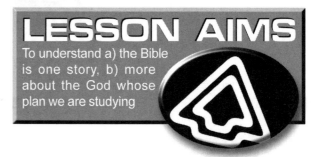

LESSON AIMS

To understand a) the Bible is one story, b) more about the God whose plan we are studying

Genesis means 'origins' or 'beginnings'. The creation stories found at the beginning of Genesis are foundational to our understanding of who God is, who we are and why our world is as it is. Christians have sometimes avoided studying these chapters, because the science issue and disagreements between Christians as to whether the creation account should be understood literally or figuratively can make us nervous. However, this is God's revelation about himself and we must start where he starts. We do well to let these chapters speak for themselves and shape our thinking about God rather than try to make them answer our questions or support a particular point of view.

1:1	'In the beginning God' - God was there in the beginning. He has always existed and he created everything out of nothing.
1:2	The earth was 'formless' and 'empty'.
1:3-13	These verses show how God created 'form' in our world out of formlessness, order out of chaos. The world was brought into being by God's word. Each step required a creative act of God so each step begins with a word of God.
1:3	And God said .... the first day.
1:6	And God said .... the second day.
1:9	And God said ....
1:11	Then God said .... the third day. On the third day God speaks twice, indicating that there was no spontaneous 'evolution' of elements to living plants. The beginning of life was a creative act of God.

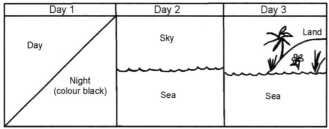

Day 1	Day 2	Day 3
Day / Night (colour black)	Sky / Sea	Land / Sea

1:14-31	These verses tell us how God filled the 'emptiness'. The pattern seen in the first 3 days is repeated.
1:14	And God said .... the fourth day.
1:20	And God said .... the fifth day.
1:24	And God said ....
1:26	Then God said .... the sixth day. On the sixth day, as on the third day, God speaks twice. This indicates that there was no spontaneous 'evolution' of mankind from animals. The creating of mankind was a separate creative act of God and was the climax of creation.

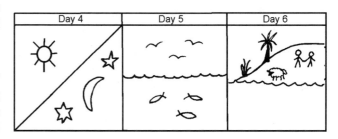

Day 4	Day 5	Day 6

The things God created in days 4-6 fill the structures created in days 1-3:   day 4 filling day 1

day 5 filling day 2

day 6 filling day 3.

2:2-3	God rested. This is important; the creation culminated in rest. God did not rest because he was worn out but because the creation was finished. The goal of creation had been achieved. We will meet the theme of rest during this course so it is important to draw attention to it here.

What does this tell us about God?

♦ He was there at the beginning - he was not himself created.

♦ He made everything out of nothing.

♦ He is more than one. We have God, the Spirit of God (v.2) and the Word of God active in creation.

♦ He is orderly and purposeful in his creating. He forms the world then fills it.

What does this tell us about ourselves?

♦ We are special; we are made in the image of God. We are like God in all kinds of ways. As we look at each other we see creativeness, management, relationships and speech and we are reminded of God.

♦ We are not the same as animals. The making of man was a separate creative act.

♦ Men and women are equally created in God's image.

♦ We were made to take responsibility for our world and rule over it as God rules over the whole of Creation.

What does it tell us about our world?

♦ Creation seems to be made ultimately for man (this is made clearer in the Eden narrative in ch.2).

♦ It was very good (1:10,12,18,21,25,31).

♦ It was finished (we should not expect further development).

♦ Our world was not formed by accident; it was formed and filled by the will of God.

♦ There was no spontaneous evolution of living things.

♦ Sun, moon and stars are not gods and do not control us. They were created by God just like us. (This is less of a problem to us than to previous generations, but astrology is still an issue in our society.)

Lesson Summary

God created the world out of nothing. He did it in an orderly and purposeful way and everything he made was good. The climax of his creation was the making of mankind in his image. The goal of creation was rest.

The creation tells us much about what God is like and helps us to understand ourselves and the world we live in.

What Story?

Prior to the session select 6 books that are familiar to the group and copy out a paragraph or two from the middle of each one onto separate pieces of paper. Number the papers from 1 to 6 and stick them up around the room. Divide the group into twos or threes and ask them to try and guess from which books the story excerpts come and what part of the story is being portrayed. The winner is the small group which gets the most right.

Point out that this is not generally how we read a book and may lead us to totally misunderstand the story. Yet if we already know the story (as some of them will) it is not a problem to dip in and out like this.

1. Focus activity.

2. Prior to the lesson write a very short story, consisting of a couple of sentences, about something amusing or embarassing that has happened to you. Write out each word of the story on separate pieces of paper and give the individual words to the group in order. Get the group to read out the story, one word at a time.

   Although the story came in different parts, read by different people, it was all part of one story, written by the same person. It's much the same with the Bible, where we see God's one story.

   The Bible is actually one story, just like the novel, different in that it's true, but one story nevertheless. However, when we study the Bible we often study individual passages without being really clear about the whole story. This series is all about understanding the whole story of the Bible.

   Use a jigsaw, in pieces, in a box. Pick out one piece (carefully selected in advance) and ask the group to describe it and guess the picture from which it comes. How would they find out whether or not they were right? Look at the picture on the box to see how right they were. When you can see the whole picture it is much easier to understand what you are looking at on the individual pieces. When we study the Bible we tend to look at individual stories and passages like examining individual bits of a jigsaw. To have the whole story of the Bible in our minds is like being able to visualise the picture on the box. This makes it much, much easier to fit the individual Bible stories together and understand what is there.

3. Photocopy the Bible passage for each group member. Supply felt tip or highlighter pens. Read the passage and establish what things were like at the beginning.

   Get them to highlight or underline all the 'And/ Then God said' phrases in one colour and the 'Day' phrases in another. This will make it easy for them to see the pattern.

4. Get them to highlight what was made on each day using the same colour for days 1 & 4 , 2 & 5 and 3 & 6. This makes clear the forming and filling pattern.

   And/or draw the days of creation chart (see page 10) and then fill it. This is best done as a group activity.

5. Go through the 3 'What does this tell us about …?' questions, eliciting the answers from group members. You may need to help by giving verse numbers or clues. Be prepared to supply some of the answers. Summarise the answers on a board or flipchart.

PREPARATION

Genesis 2:4-25, Revelation 21:1-4; 21:22-22:5

LESSON AIMS

To understand a) life in Eden was God's plan for mankind and will be restored b) people are different from animals and have a unique relationship with God.

The account of creation as revealed in Genesis 2 is different from that revealed in Genesis 1. Whilst the focus in Genesis 1 is on the forming and filling of the world, in Genesis 2 the focus is on the place of human beings within God's creation. Genesis 2 expands on the revelation given in 1:26-31 about the creation of people. It also gives us a clear picture of how life was at the beginning in God's perfect world, something the Bible refers to subsequently as a state of rest.

NB These do not appear to be the same account, but they describe the same events from different viewpoints. They are not contradictory, but blend together.

The New Testament leaves us in no doubt that Adam and Eve were real people, who lived, not mythical characters (Romans 5:12-14, 1 Corinthians 15:45-49, 1 Timothy 2:13-14).

Genesis

2:4-7   The focus of this passage is the creation of the man, Adam. He is made from the 'dust of the earth' (the elements), just like everything else in creation. What makes him different is that God has breathed into him the breath of life.

2:8-9   God created a garden for the man, a paradise for him to enjoy and benefit from. The emphasis here is not on Man being one of God's creatures, but on creation being made around him and for him. Mankind is the most important part of creation. This is implied in chapter 1 but made very explicit in this passage.

The garden was a beautiful place, full of life. In the middle of it was the tree of life along with the tree of the knowledge of good and evil. We are not told very much about the nature of these trees, but we know that eating from the tree of life led to eternal life (3:22) and eating from the tree of the knowledge of Good and Evil would result in death (2:17). The Tree of Life recurs later in the Bible and is important.

2:10-14   The rivers watering the garden are also important. They arise in Eden and flow out to the whole world. Eden and what happens there will bless the whole world.

This pattern of rivers flowing out from God's special place and God's special relationship with his people overflowing to bless the whole world is a theme we encounter again and again throughout the Bible, so it is worth drawing attention to it here where we first meet it. The rivers Tigris and Euphrates have been well known since ancient times. The actual course of the Pishon and Gihon rivers is not known.

2:15-17   We see here what life was like in God's perfect world for Adam. He was put in the garden by God and was given a job to do. Adam worked in the garden caring for what God had created. This is very much a parallel passage to 1:28-30. We see the man ruling over what God has made.

Adam was under God's authority, but it was voluntary. Unlike the commands of God we saw in Chapter 1, where everything obeyed God's word of command, God's command to Adam was able to be resisted. It required Adam's obedience. This shows how different God's relationship with him was compared with the rest of creation. No other creature was called to live under God's authority in this way.

Adam lived in uninterrupted fellowship with God (made clearer in 3:8).

2:18-24   This difference from other creatures is further emphasised in these verses. Adam was given responsibility for naming the animals.

No animal was a suitable companion for the Man; only one of his own kind would do. Adam's delight at Eve's creation makes this plain. The introduction of the concept of marriage at this point further underlines the delightfulness of this relationship.

2:25 Adam and Eve felt no shame at their nakedness, because in the pre-fall world nothing was shameful, all was pure.

The next lesson will look at how this perfect world was spoilt by sin. Now we will look at the end of the Bible to see how the promised new creation bears a strong resemblance to the description we have of Eden in Genesis 2.

In Revelation 21:1-4; 21:22 - 22:5 we see that God will make a new creation, a new heaven and a new earth, which replaces the old, fallen one.

There will be a restoration of uninterrupted face-to-face fellowship between God and his people. No temple will be needed (v.22).

There will be no death or crying or pain. Those things belong to the fallen world which has passed away.

The river flows from the throne of God.

The tree of life is present also.

The servants of God rule forever under God's authority.

Lesson Summary

The account of life in Eden tells us that mankind was at the centre of God's creation. He is different from all animals. He was made to live in relationship with God and, under God's authority, to rule over the creation. In Eden Adam and Eve lived in the beautiful place God had made for them in unhindered fellowship with him. Life was very good.

One day God will restore his creation, bringing back a kind of 'Eden' for his people to enjoy, which can never be spoilt by sin.

Put it Back Together

Before the session begins make a structure out of lego or building blocks or something similar. Remember how you made it. Give the group a couple of minutes to look at it then break it up into its component parts. Set the group the challenge of rebuilding the structure. Ideally, they will not be able to do it. After they have been trying for a bit, take over and do it for them.

Genesis tells us that God made his world perfect and, although it is clearly not perfect now, God will rebuild his world perfectly one day.

Lesson Plan

1. Focus activity.

2. Play a hangman game to produce the words 'Formless' and 'Empty'. Using these words get the group to remember how the world was formed and filled.

   On a large sheet of paper write down what they have remembered about what the creation account tells us about God, ourselves and our world. Prompt them if necessary to ensure that the important things are remembered.

   Ask what happened on the 7th day and why? This week's lesson looks more closely at what it means to live in God's rest.

3. After reading and asking some general questions about the passage, get the group to draw a diagram of the garden, including the river, the 2 trees, who/what was there, etc.(see below). Write in the garden what was not there, e.g. no shame, no sin, no clothes.

   Start off with something like this and add to it.

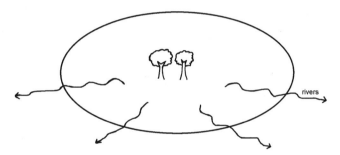

4. Discuss what the world is like now and why.

5. Introduce the Revelation passage as, 'what the world will be like once again'. After reading it, ask what the restored creation will be like? Tick or underline the elements on the diagram of Eden as they recur.

6. Go back to the sheet of paper filled in at the beginning of the lesson with what they had learned about God, ourselves and our world. Add the new information learned about these things from our study of Eden.

PREPARATION
Genesis 3:1-24

LESSON AIMS

To learn that sin affected all of creation, including God's relationship with his people.

For a 26 session course on the whole Bible, it may seem excessive to spend the first 3 lessons studying just 3 chapters. However, these chapters are central to our understanding of everything that follows in the Bible. Laying our foundations carefully is time well spent. In the last study we saw that God's intention for mankind was that they should live as rulers of his world, in relationship with him, under his authority and in the place that he provided. The Bible refers to this situation as 'rest'. Adam and Eve expressed their willingness to live under God's authority by keeping the rule God had given them. It was right that they lived under God's authority, because God is the maker of the world and therefore owns it. It is his. God expected people to keep his command as a matter of free choice and not compulsion, so there was always a possibility that they would rebel and reject God's rule over them, which, of course, is what happened next.

3:1 The tempter, who is Satan, takes the form of a serpent. Rebellion against God is already a reality in the spiritual realms. He encourages Eve to doubt God's word.

3:2-3 Eve affirms God's rule, but adds to it something of her own. This is not a good sign!

3:4 The serpent denies that the result of breaking God's law will be death. He actively denies God's word concerning judgment.

3:5 He encourages Eve to doubt God's goodness. He tells her that God is withholding something good from her, therefore he is not good.

3:6 Eve follows her own desires and rejects God's authority over her. Her view of God seems to have been altered by the serpent's lies.

3:7 Adam follows Eve and by his disobedience sin entered the world. That day Adam and Eve made a choice; they chose not to trust in God's goodness nor to trust that God's words are true, but to make their own judgments regarding their own well-being.

In effect, they rebelled against God's right to be in authority over them. As they made that choice something in them changed forever. They felt shame that they were unable to hide. They were no longer at ease with one another...

3:8 ...or with God.

3:12-14 Adam blames his wife for what has happened and Eve blames the serpent. God had made the man to rule, the woman to help and the creatures to be ruled by them. Here is a remarkable inverting of the God-given pattern - the serpent tells the woman what to do and the woman tells the man.

The curses

3:14-15 To the serpent. There will now be enmity between people and snakes, but the change signified by this curse is probably more far-reaching than that. People will no longer exercise dominion over animals as God intended. It will no longer be a benign rule, but there will be enmity and struggle.

At another level this is a promise that one day a human will arise who will crush the serpent's head - ie. defeat Satan. This is the first signpost in the Old Testament which points to Jesus.

3:16 To the woman. She will experience an increase of pain and difficulty in childbirth and in her relationship with her husband.

3:17-19 To the man. The work God has given him will become difficult and frustrating. Not only have Adam and Eve changed as a result of their rebellion, but the whole of creation has become subject to decay (Romans 8:18-21). Thorns and weeds are now part of it, as is disease and, ultimately, death. Adam will die and return to the ground. God's words of judgment were true.

3:22 Adam and Eve were driven out of Eden.

They would not be allowed to eat from the tree of life and live forever; they would die. No longer could they have fellowship with God; they had rebelled and become God's enemies. The consequences or rebellion against God has always been separation from him. No longer would Adam and Eve be at the centre of God's plan for blessing the whole world.

Lesson Summary

Adam and Eve were not compelled to live under God's authority. First they doubted that God's word was good for them and then they disobeyed it, taking themselves out from under the authority of God. As they did this the whole world changed. They were cursed by God, so that their everyday lives were filled with frustration and difficulty. Their relationships with God and with each other were spoiled. No longer were they capable of ruling over the creation - it had changed, too, and everything became a struggle. They were cast out of the garden forever and death became their inevitable end.

Headliners

Either, cut out some 'bad news' headlines from recent newspapers and cover up one of the words in each headline. Ask the group to guess the missing word. This can be done as a group or individually as a competition. Or, hand out a number of newspapers and get the group to cut out as many 'bad news' headlines as they can find. Stick them up onto a board or wall. Point out that all these headlines make it clear that the world we live in is a long way from the perfect world that God created, (and which we have been looking at in Genesis 1 & 2). Today we will find out what went wrong.

Lesson Plan

1. Focus activity.

2. In recapping introduce the Eden diagram (see below), which will be used in different forms throughout the course.

   a) God made the world and everything in it.

   b) The climax was the creation of mankind, made in God's own image.

   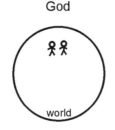

   c) These people were to have a unique role, to rule over the earth and subdue it, and a unique relationship with God.

   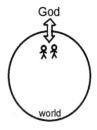

   d) The first man and woman were called Adam and Eve. God placed them in a special place, Eden, where they were able to live with and communicate freely with God. Their willingness to accept God's authority over them was expressed by keeping the command that God had given them.

   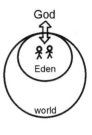

   e) Eden and what happened there was to bring blessing to the whole world, (pictured here as rivers flowing out from Eden). Eden is the ideal situation for God's people: - living in the place God has provided, - living under God's authority, - bringing blessing to the whole world.

   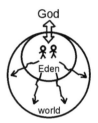

   The Bible refers to this situation as 'rest'.

3. Read the passage as a dramatic Bible reading with group members taking different parts. This is easier if you photocopy the text and underline the parts in advance.

4. Study the passage, drawing attention particularly to how Eve came to break God's rule and exploring what was going through her mind as she made her choices. Do this for Adam also.

5. On a flipchart or large sheet of paper, write down the consequences of the Fall, including the curses. How do we see these expressed in our world today? You could organise this in the 3 columns that we have used before: God, Ourselves, The World.

6. Look at any evidence for God's continued care, e.g. the promise of 3:15, the coverings of animal skins. You could also discuss whether exclusion from the tree of life was merciful, not allowing them to live in a state of separation from God forever.

Week 4
A New Start and a Familiar Ending

PREPARATION
Genesis 4 - 11

LESSON AIMS
To see how sin developed in the world and how big a problem this posed.

This study is an overview of the rest of Biblical prehistory from the birth of Cain and Abel to the Tower of Babel. It tracks the development of sin from Cain to the general wickedness preceeding the Flood. It shows how the new start provided by the flood failed to provide a solution to sin. Mankind was as rebellious as ever, demonstrated by the arrogance of those building the Tower of Babel.

Genesis 4-5

Adam and Eve have 2 sons. Sin in the life of Cain leads him to murder Abel. Six generations later we have Lamech, who revels in murder (4:19-24). But there is still hope. The birth of Seth represents a new, 'clean' line of decendants of Adam and Eve. This is the 'line' the Bible writer chooses to follow in 4:25 - 5:32. After everyone, except Enoch, we get the words 'and then he died'. This emphasises that death is the inescapable consequence of sin.

Genesis 6-11

6:1-4   These verses are difficult and contentious. There are 3 main theories concerning who these 'sons of God' may be.

a) They may be heavenly beings, who became flesh rather than pure spirit and who had sexual relations with humans.

b) They may be men from the line of Seth the godly or 'clean' line, who intermarried with the ungodly line of Cain.

c) They may be local kings, who were thought of as sons of 'gods'.

All these theories have problems, so avoid talking about these verses if you can. They add very little to the big picture.

6:5-7   This describes how thoroughly wicked mankind had become as a result of their rebellion against God. 'Every inclination of the thoughts of his heart was only evil all the time.' You cannot get worse than that and God's response is equally chilling. 'The Lord was grieved that he had made man on the earth and his heart was filled with pain.' This contrasts markedly with what God said when he first created people, 'God saw all that he had made and it was very good' (1:31). It shows us clearly the seriousness of sin.

6:8-9   But there is still hope. Noah walks with God, a term reminiscent of God walking in the Garden in Genesis 3 and used in the Bible only of Noah and Enoch. Noah is described as righteous and blameless; he finds favour in the eyes of the Lord. He is not perfect; he is still sinful. Here we see an example of God's grace. God **chose** to rescue Noah. Chapter 5 shows that he was from the line of Seth.

6:18-21   God talks of establishing his covenant with Noah. A covenant was a contract between 2 parties where each party was bonded together in a formal relationship. The covenant set out what was required from each party and what would happen if the covenant was broken. In OT times there were 2 types of covenant or treaty -

1. A suzerainty or vassal covenant was one between an overlord (or great king) and a subject person or nation.

2. A parity covenant was one between equals, e.g. David and Jonathan (1 Samuel 20:12-17,42).

The covenant God made with his people was a suzerainty covenant. To simplify matters we will call this type a covenant and the parity covenant a contract. The covenants God made with his people were one-sided arrangements. One party decides to give something to another party, as in a Will. Despite overwhelming sin, God is still commited to mankind. He is going to make a way of salvation through the judgment he is bringing on the earth. This will be available to Noah and his family.

7:5   Noah's outstanding qualities are shown by his willingness to do what God had told him, despite there being no visible evidence that a flood was imminent. The story of the flood is well known and does not need to be studied, just remembered. It proves that God is willing to judge those who rebel against him. He is so grieved by human wickedness that he is prepared to wipe out his own creation. We should be left in no doubt that he will judge and destroy our world, as he has promised, in order to establish a New Heaven and a New Earth (2 Peter 3:5-7).

9:1-3   This repeats Chapter 1.It seems to indicate that this is a new beginning for mankind and the world. Will it be the restoration of God's 'rest'? Has the situation described in Eden been restored?

9:18-25   These verses show us that, although the world has been made new, the heart of man is still sinful. The problem of sin and rebellion has not been wiped out by the flood.

9:26-27   This hints that the line of Canaan is now considered as unclean. Later we find the line of Shem, the Semites, picked out as the godly line.

11:1-4   The story of the Tower of Babel shows us that rejection of God's authority is again rife. The builders of the tower demonstrate the same attitude as Adam and Eve in the Garden of Eden. They grasp at equality with God, as by their own efforts they try to reach the heavens. They want to make their name great. (This is important for the next study.) They decide to group together rather than to be scattered throughout the earth (cf. 9:1). They decide to sideline God and make themselves great.

11:5-8   This demonstrates the brilliance of mankind made in God's image, as well as his limitations. Our world is full of the obvious consequences of this confusion of languages in the inabilty of different people groups to co-operate with one another. The arrogance displayed here also remains endemic in our world and we still see tensions between different nations acting as a restraint on man's ambitions.

So all children decended from Adam and Eve were born rebels, even those from Noah's family. A new start for the earth was not the answer, because the problem of sin travelled in the Ark with Noah and his family. A different kind of new start is needed.

Lesson Summary

Life for Adam and Eve's descendants outside the garden was full of death and wickedness. By the time of Noah it had got so offensive to God that he wiped out the world and everyone in it with a flood, saving only a righteous man and his family to make a new start. However, even though the world was new, human nature had not changed, so it was not long before the sin in the lives of Noah and his family became apparent. As the population increased, sin once again gathered momentum, culminating in the breathtaking arrogance of the Tower of Babel. A new start for the world was not the answer to sin.

Spread It

Play a game of tag, starting with one person as 'It'. However, when someone is caught that person joins the catcher as 'It'. Very soon everyone will be caught.

If you do not have much space, you can illustrate the same point by playing a version of wink murder. One person in the group is the murderer and winks at people to murder them. However, when a person is winked at, instead of dying, he/she becomes a murderer as well. Very quickly everyone will become murderers.

This game demonstrates how quickly sin spreads, as we shall see in these chapters in Genesis.

1. Focus activity.

2. Recap on the Eden situation by using the diagram. Get the group to remember all the things that have changed as a result of the Fall. Draw a new diagram representing the new situation. Has God washed his hands of Adam and Eve, or does he still care for them?

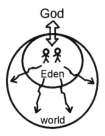

3. This lesson covers a lot of ground which will be familiar to the young people. Ask them to flick through Genesis 4-11 and write down the main events. Read 6:5-7 and discuss how things got that bad by referring to the events which come before it.

4. Focus on Noah. Read 6:8-22. What does this tell us about Noah? What does God promise to do? What does this tell us about God?

5. Read 8:18 - 9:16. What does God promise and what does he command? Draw attention to the words in 9:1 and where we have seen them before. This is a new start for the world. Will it turn out better this time? Why?

Talk about what happened next, (Noah's drunkeness), and how things went from bad to worse, ending with the Tower of Babel.

6. Read 11:1-9. Focus on how the attitude of the men of Babel was similar to that of Adam and Eve. Draw attention to the fact that, by gathering together, they were disobeying the command to fill the earth.

7. Make a tower with hymn books or similar items, e.g. plastic cups, matchboxes, etc. Group members take it in turns to add to the pile. As they place a book onto the top they have to say a 'sin'. Anyone who repeats a sin or knocks over the tower is out. Point out that, in the end, all evil and everything that opposes God will be destroyed.

PREPARATION
Genesis 12:1-7; 15:1-21; 17:1-22

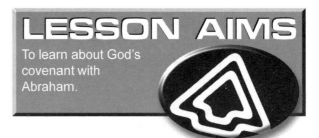

LESSON AIMS
To learn about God's covenant with Abraham.

In the previous 2 studies we have seen that sin is a huge problem. It is not just doing 'wrong things', but is an attitude which rejects God's authority and says, 'I'll do things my way, not God's way.' Sin makes God and man enemies.

All this makes the next part of the Bible story truly remarkable. God picks out Abraham, who is just an ordinary, sinful man. He does not deserve God's special favour and is not any more fit to be in God's presence than Adam and Eve were. Yet God calls him and makes an extraordinary covenant with him and his descendants. Clearly, God has not washed his hands of mankind.

These promises made to Abraham are of enormous importance. Essentially they are promises to take Abraham's descendants back to a situation like Eden. The whole of the Old Testament, from Genesis 12 onwards, has these promises, which were made to Abraham, in view.

11:10-32 This passage tells us that Abraham came from the 'clean' line of Noah's son, Shem.

12:1-7 The Covenant made with Abraham

12:1 Ur of the Chaldeans, where Abraham came from, was the centre of the civilisation of the day. Abraham was being asked to leave not only his family, but a developed, probably pagan, culture, and set out in a new direction with God. The sequence of events is made clearer in Acts 7:2-4.

12:2-3 Here we have a first look at the promises made to Abraham.

1. Abraham will have many descendants and become a great nation.

2. He will enjoy a special relationship of blessing with God.

3. All people on earth will be blessed through Abraham.

God says, 'I will make your name great,' which contrasts with the builders of Babel, who said, 'Let us make a name for ourselves.' God is going to bestow greatness on Abraham in his way.

12:4-5 Abraham obeyed. We see his willingness to have God in charge of his life.

12:6-7 The inferred promise of a land in v.1 is made explicit here. God promises to give Abraham's offspring this land.

15:1-19 The Confirmation and the Covenant made with Abraham

15:1-3 Abraham has a problem with these promises. He has no children, so how can he become a great nation?

15:4-5 God reassures him concerning this promise and adds to it. The fulfilment of the promise will come about via an heir from Abraham's own body, his physical child.

15:6 It would not have been easy for an elderly, childless man to believe God's promises, but he did. 'Abram believed the LORD and he credited it to him as righteousness.' This phrase is picked up and explained more fully by Paul in Romans 4 and Galatians 3:6.

15:7-11 God reiterates his promise of the land and confirms his covenant with Abraham with a formal ceremony. Cutting animals in half and walking down the middle of them signifies the seriousness of the covenant. The parties involved are swearing allegiance to one another. They are saying to one another, 'May we end up like these animals if we break our word.'

15:12-16 Abraham is told it will be 400 years, or 4 generations (probably meaning 4 life-spans), before the land will belong to his descendants, during which time they will experience hardship (clearly predicting the time they would spend in Egypt).

15:17-21 It is significant that only God, (in the form of a brazier and a torch), walks between the animal pieces. This covenant with Abraham is unilateral. It is not a mutual agreement, but much more like a will, where God decides the terms and God makes the promises. God adds more details to the promises regarding the land he will give to Abraham's descendants.

In chapter 16 Abraham shows that familiar tendency, shared by all sinful humans, to doubt God's promise and make his own arrangements for offspring. He has a son by his wife's maidservant.

17:1-22 **God reconfirms the Covenant and gives a sign**

17:1-2   This event happens 24 years after the original promise in chapter 12.

17:3-6   God reiterates his promise concerning offspring and makes it clear that his covenant will be established, not through Hagar's child, but through a child born to Abraham and Sarah in their old age.

17:7-8   The covenant will last forever; God will be the God of Abraham and his descendants forever. The land he is giving them will be theirs forever. (Hebrews 11:8-10 gives an interesting perspective on this.)

17:9-13 Circumcision is given as a sign of the covenant.

17:14   This is the first indication that this covenant has some obligations for the covenant people.

17:23-27 Abraham obeys God and circumcises his household.

Abraham shows himself to be a man of great faith throughout his life. There is no more striking example of this than his willingness to obey God and sacrifice his miracle son Isaac at God's command (Genesis 22). He must have believed still that God would keep his promise and perhaps even bring Isaac back to life (Hebrews 11:17-19).

Isaac's children were the twins, Esau and Jacob. Again, we see God picking out one of them to be the inheritor of the promises. God chose Seth's line, then Shem's and now Jacob's. Jacob had 12 sons and so we see the promise of a great nation taking a stride forward. Jacob was given the name 'Israel' after he had wrestled with God. The name Israel means 'he struggles with God'. It is an apt name as we see God's chosen people continually struggling with him throughout their history.

Lesson Summary

God had not washed his hands of mankind, but was prepared to make another new start. He initiates a relationship with a man called Abraham, telling him to leave his home and go to the land God will show him. God makes a covenant with Abraham declaring that he will make him into a great nation, he and his descendants will have a special relationship with God and all nations will be blessed through him. This is a promise to restore a situation very like Eden for Abraham and his descendants. God intervenes in a miraculous way to give him and his wife in their old age a son, who will be the heir of the promises. These promises form the basis for God's dealings with his people, the Israelites, (children of Abraham's grandchild Jacob, also called Israel), throughout the Old Testament.

Promises, Promises

Everybody in the group has to make a promise to do something specific and beneficial for another member of the group by the end of the session. Get everyone to write down the promise on a piece of paper, stating who they are, what they will do and who for. Collect up the pieces of paper and tell the group that you will read them out at the end of the session and find out who has kept their promises.

Today we will learn about a promise God made to Abraham.

1.   Focus activity.

2.   Start to make the Bible timeline (pages 83-86). Do this as a joint activity, using a long piece of wallpaper or similar that can be attached to a board or wall. Ask some of the group members to cut out the 4 pre-history images from page 86. Draw in the Eden diagram in the Bible book column. (Group members can make individual timelines if desired. Photocopy the timeline pages 80 - 82 for each group member.) Ask questions about what these events have taught us about God, ourselves and our world. Focus particularly on the intractability of sin and the enmity between man and God that it creates.

3.   Go through the Genesis 12 passage in detail and study the promises given to Abraham. Draw attention to what an amazingly gracious and unexpected intervention of God this was in the light of the events studied in previous weeks.

     Make sure they understand what a covenant is. Remind them of the covenant made with Noah and his descendants in the previous study.

     Some explanation of the covenant ritual in chapter 15 would be helpful.

4.   Make a chart of the promises, using the headings: Descendants, Land, Special Relationship.

     Read through the other passages and see how each confirms or enlarges on the original promises, adding to the chart. Add ticks to confirmed or restated promises. Write down any new promises or additions to existing promises. These promises can be relabelled, in a more memorable way, as:

     • God's People (the many descendants of Abraham)

     • In God's Place (the promised land)

- Under God's authority (implied in the special relationship).

Remind them that, through this special relationship between Abraham's descendants and God, the whole world will be blessed.

Write down Abraham's obligations towards God. (NB It is quite common to find that young people of this age do not have a clue as to what circumcision involves and are grateful for an explanation.)

5. Draw a new version of the 'Eden' diagram and point out that what is being promised is in some ways a promise of restoration of something like Eden.

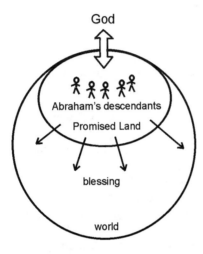

This was not just for the benefit of Abraham and his descendants, but would be a blessing to the whole world.

6. Flick through the rest of Genesis, writing down the main events.

7. Read out the promises from the Focus Activity and find out who has kept them.

PREPARATION
Genesis 50:22-26;
Exodus 1:1 - 2:25

LESSON AIMS
To understand that God had not forgotten his covenant with Abraham.

Nearly 400 years pass between the end of Genesis and the beginning of Exodus. For all that time Jacob's descendants have been living in safety and relative prosperity in Egypt. The next big chunk of Bible history is centred around Moses and the escape from Egypt. These events are of enormous importance, because they concern the founding of the nation of Israel. In this study we see that God has not forgotten the promises he made to Abraham (see Exodus 2:24).

Genesis

50:22-26 This shows Joseph's faith in God's promises to Abraham. He wants his bones to be taken to the promised land of Canaan when God fulfils his promise. (Joseph's bones feature later in the Exodus narrative.)

Exodus

1:1-7 Picks up the story from Genesis 46 with the 70 descendants of Jacob, who left Canaan for Egypt. God has not yet fulfilled his promise to bring them back to the land he has promised them. However, God is blessing them by making them very numerous so that they fill the land. (Here are echoes of Genesis 1:28 and 9:1.)

1:8-22 **Oppression under a new King**

There were so many Israelites that the new king considered them a threat to his rule. He decides to oppress them in order to reduce the threat. The oppression comes in three phases:

1. Slave labour.
2. A secret plan to kill male children via the midwives.
3. Open slaughter of Hebrew male children.

The King's policy did not work.

1:12 The more the Israelites were oppressed, the more they multiplied.

1:20 The people increased and became even more numerous. Under normal circumstances poor treatment would result in a decline in population, but God had promised to make Abraham's descendants into a great nation. This fruitfulness of the Israelites was caused by God keeping that promise. Not even Pharaoh, the most powerful ruler of his day, can stand in the way of God's promises.

The midwives are puzzling. They have Hebrew names, but Pharaoh seems to expect them to co-operate with him rather than with the Hebrews, which may suggest that they were Egyptian. Also, can there really only have been 2 midwives for such a large population? (According to Numbers there were over 600,000 men aged 20 years and over, who left at the time of the Exodus.) The midwives seem to be held up as examples of those whose fear of God was impressive, rather like Rahab in Joshua 2. This would fit better with them being Egyptian.

1:22 This sets the scene for the birth of one Hebrew child in particular - Moses.

2:1-10 The story of Moses' birth is very well known, however, some things about it need to be emphasised.

Moses' family saw something in this child, which made them willing to defy Pharaoh's command (Hebrews 11:23). This shows some evidence of faith in God being exercised by this family.

Moses was put in the Nile, just like other Hebrew babies, but he was rescued. This was partly due to the actions of his mother and of Pharaoh's daughter, but it is clear that God is in control of the whole situation. Moses is the one whom God has picked out to be the rescuer of his people.

Pharaoh ordered this evil act in order to make himself and his nation more secure. It is ironic that he ends up raising in his own household the one whom God will use to bring about what he most fears, the downfall of his nation. It shows clearly that Pharaoh is not in control - God is.

God has arranged things so perfectly that Moses is able to be cared for by his own mother and thus gain some appreciation of his Hebrew background.

2:11-12 This shows how, despite being raised as an Egyptian, Moses identifies with his own people.

2:13-14 But the Hebrews do not identify with him. There is more irony here, as they say, 'Who made you ruler and judge over us?' This is exactly what Moses becomes in time. No comment is made about the rights or wrongs of Moses' action.

2:15 Moses runs away from the wrath of Pharaoh and goes to Midian (modern day NW Saudi Arabia and S Jordan). This is quite a long way.

2:16-22 Moses seems to fare well in Midian, marrying into the family of the priest of Midian. However, in the naming of his son 'Gershom' we see a cry of discomfort, 'I have become an alien in a foreign land'. He would have felt very at home in Egypt, most of his upbringing having been Egyptian. Now he feels the same kind of alienation as God's people feel. God is using Moses' time in Midian to prepare him for the task God has for him. He is learning to identify with God's people in their longing for their own land.

2:23-25 Pharaoh dies, but the oppression of God's people goes on. God's people cry out for help in their distress and God hears them and remembers his promises. This does not imply that, up to this point, the covenant had slipped his mind. Rather, when the Bible says, God remembers his promises, it means that God is acting to fulfil his promises.

In a bleak period of Israel's history we can still see God at work:

♦ Against all odds his people remain fruitful.

♦ He acts with kindness towards the midwives.

♦ He raises up a rescuer and starts to train him for the job.

♦ He hears the cries of his people and is concerned for them.

♦ He prepares to act on his promises.

Genesis 15:13-14 predicts this period of Israel's history and ties it tightly to the promises made to Abraham. This oppression is not evidence that God has forgotten his promises, rather, it is the precursor of fulfilment.

Lesson Summary

400 years after Israel's family settled in Egypt they are still there. They are being oppressed and used as slave labour by the King of the Egyptians, but God has not forgotten his promises. He is making them into a great nation - their population is growing. He has heard their cries of distress and is preparing to act on his promises by raising up a rescuer whom he will use to deliver them.

FOCUS ACTIVITY

Broken Promises

Get the group to think about times when they have broken promises they have made, or when people have broken promises to them. Ask them to feed their experiences back to the group. Discuss how they felt when promises were broken.

This introduces the idea of broken promises. The Israelites were in trouble. Had God forgotten his promises?

Lesson Plan

1. Focus activity.

2. Get the group to fill in the blanks.

God promised Abraham that:

♦ he would be a g _ _ _ _ n _ _ _ _ _ _ , (great nation)

♦ he will enjoy a s _ _ _ _ _ _ r _ _ _ _ _ _ _ _ _ _ with God, (special relationship)

♦ God will give him a _ _ _ _ for his descendents, (land)

♦ all nations will be _ _ _ _ _ _ _ through Abraham. (blessed)

Also get them to remember: God's People, in God's Place, under God's Authority. Ask the group where we have seen these 3 come together before? (Eden) So what Abraham is being promised is the Eden situation restored.

Make a Family Tree with blank spaces to lead the group to Joseph (see page 88).

Where were Joseph's family at the end of Genesis? Why were they there?

3. This is a manageable length passage, so can be run as an ordinary Bible study.

4. It is important to make sure that the main thrust of the passage is not lost in the detail.

The things the group has learned from the study can be summarised by 3 headings:

♦ Focus on the Covenant (How does Israel's current situation measure up against the promises made to Abraham? How do we know that God has not forgotten?)

♦ Focus on Moses (What indications do we have that Moses is special?)

♦ Focus on God (What do we learn about God in this passage?)

5. If you have time, add Abraham and slavery to the timeline. (Timeline Pages 81-87)

PREPARATION

Exodus 3:1 - 4:31

LESSON AIMS

To understand that Moses was God's chosen rescuer.

In the last session we saw how God picked out a man through whom he would rescue his people. Interestingly, Moses was saved through water, like Noah, and put by God in a position of influence, like Joseph. In due time God revealed himself to Moses. This study is about how God did that and equipped Moses for his part in God's plan, to lead God's people out of slavery in Egypt to the land he had promised them.

Although their slavery and oppression is the most obvious thing God's people need to be rescued from, it is not the only issue for God. His plan is to restore the pattern of Eden. God wants his chosen people to be living in the place he has provided, under his authority. These 3 things are not separate, but related to one another. It is very difficult for God's people to be distinctive when living within another nation. It is very difficult for them to be under God's authority - to truly have him as their God - when all around are pagan gods and pagan practices. What they need is a land of their own, where they can live as a distinct nation, a place where they can serve God properly, without any pagan distractions.

3:1 Mt Horeb (also known as Mt Sinai) is in the south of the Sinai Desert, which is a long way from Midian (see map on page 79).

3:2-4 Although what Moses saw was a burning bush, not God in person, clearly what is happening here is God appearing to Moses.

3:5-6 God introduces himself to Moses as the God of Abraham, Isaac and Jacob, the Covenant God, the God who makes promises and keeps them. Moses also learns that God is holy (v.5), awesome (v.6), a speaking God and he knows Moses by name (v.4). This may be familiar to us, but Moses was a man who, though he knew something of his Hebrew roots, had spent 40 years in Egyptian high society and then 40 years in the deserts of Midian.

3:7-10 God sets out his plan to rescue Israel and fulfil his promises. He is going to use Moses to accomplish it. In these verses many other things about God are communicated: he sees, he hears, he is concerned for his people (v.7), he has come down, he is going to rescue, he is going to fulfil his promises (v.8).

3:11 - 4:17 **Moses' response to his part in this plan**

He raises 5 questions or problems. He does not think he could possibly be the right man for the job. After each question God gently reassures Moses that he will be enabled for the task. However, when Moses' 5th question amounts to refusal rather than uncertainty, God's anger burns against Moses.

3:11-12 Problem 1. - Who am I?

This is an entirely reasonable question. Moses understands what a big task this is and doubts he is up to it.

The gist of God's answer seems to be, 'It doesn't matter who you are. It is who I am that matters and I will be with you.' The sign given to Moses that God has sent him is in the future. It will be given when the task has been successful. Moses is being asked to put his faith in a promise, just as Abraham was.

3:13-22 Problem 2. - Who are You?

God's answer, 'I am who I am,' could also mean 'I will be who I will be.' This is a puzzling name, but God does not explain it. Rather, he ties it to 2 things:

1. The God of the Covenant promises made to Abraham, Isaac and Jacob.

2. The God who is going to act in the way described.

   Through these actions God will demonstrate his character in a way which will be remembered from generation to generation.

4:1-9 Problem 3. - What if they will not listen?

God's answer is to give Moses 3 signs he can perform to show God's authority rests with him.

4:10-12 Problem 4. - But I cannot speak.

God's answer is, 'I made your mouth and I will help you and teach you what to say.'

4:13-17 Problem 5. - Please send someone else.

23

This is not a question, but a refusal. God's answer is that he will send someone else, but Moses is still going!

Moses is reluctant to do what God has told him to do, nevertheless he goes and, once he gives himself to the task, he proves himself to be a man of great courage, a steady leader and a good mediator.

4:18-31 **Moses returns to Egypt**

God warns Moses that there will be a struggle. God will harden Pharaoh's heart and he will not let the Israelites go. God describes Israel as his firstborn son. The judgment God will bring on Pharaoh for the mistreatment of his firstborn son is the death of Pharaoh's firstborn son.

4:24-26 Moses has to learn that, if he is going to be God's representative, he has to be obedient to all of God's commands. Circumcision was the mark of covenant membership given to all of Abraham's descendants and Moses seems to have been negligent in applying this to his own son. This was **so** serious that his own life appears to have been under threat.

4:27-31 Moses is met by Aaron at Mt Horeb. God has called Aaron also to help Moses in his task. Initially, the elders of Israel are very happy to accept both Moses' and God's words.

Lesson Summary

God's people are oppressed and need rescuing. Also they are trapped within a pagan nation and cannot properly be God's people under these circumstances. God has picked out a man whom he will use to rescue his people, taking them out of Egypt and into the land God has promised them. Before he can do this, Moses, God's rescuer, must learn about his God and be equipped for the task for which God has chosen him, and bring his own life in line with God's commands

Rescue Me!

Designate 2 areas to be a Free area and a Slaves one. Mark out a base, using chalk or rope to make a circle. One group member is the master and stands in the middle of the circle and counts to 50 with eyes closed. The remaining group members are slaves and run off to hide from the master. After counting to 50, the master leaves the base to look for his slaves. Any slave who manages to get back to the base unobserved is 'free' and sits in the Free area. Any slave who is caught sits in the Slaves area.

Slaves can be caught by:

a) the master sees them hiding, shouts, 'I see you, [slave's name],' and gets back to base before the seen slave.

b) the master sees a slave making for the base and gets there before him/her.

When any group member gets back to base before the master and goes to the Free area, all the slaves currently in the Slaves area are 'rescued' and move to the Free area.

In today's Bible study we will see how God rescued his people from slavery.

1. Focus activity.

2. Briefly recap on the promises made to Abraham. You can use the letters L, SR, GN and B as prompts.

Using the map on page 79, recap on the events of Genesis 12 onwards. Get your group to trace the route taken by the heirs of God's covenant, ending with Moses fleeing to Midian. Make sure that the group members have some idea of the part of the world where these events took place and what these countries are called today.

3. This is an ordinary Bible study, but could be structured in the following way.

Exodus 3:1-10 Moses commissioned. Remember to focus, not only on God's plan, but also on how God's character is being revealed. You can do this by making a list of the things Moses (and we, too) learns about God through this encounter.

Exodus 3:11 - 4:17 Moses' problems. Draw 5 boxes and get the group to read the passage and find the 5 problems. Write them in the boxes as they are discovered, then go through them one at a time to see how God answered each one. Add to the list of things learned about God.

Exodus 4:18-31 Moses obeys. Discuss which other ways God uses to prepare Moses for what lies ahead, e.g. Aaron's help, warning of Pharaoh's response, safety now in Egypt, the circumcision of his son.

PREPARATION

Exodus 5 - 11

LESSON AIMS

To understand that God's plan cannot be thwarted.

Israel are a disparate and oppressed minority within the most powerful nation on earth. Pharaoh is their absolute ruler. If they are ever to leave Egypt, they need to become confident in their God and sure of his power and of his care for them. The plagues are all about God showing unmistakably that the Israelites are his people and that he is more powerful than Pharaoh. God is building the confidence of his people.

5:1-2   Verse 1 may seem to us as though Moses is being economical with the truth. However, he is just repeating to Pharaoh what God has told him to say. The key statement in this passage comes in verse 2, when Pharaoh says, 'I do not know the LORD and I will not let Israel go.' This is a statement of defiance; Pharaoh is setting himself up against the God of Israel. By the end of this passage Pharaoh does indeed know the LORD and lets Israel go. Pharaoh's attitude should not surprise Moses. God has already told Moses that he will harden Pharaoh's heart and he will not let Israel go (4:21). God has told Moses that he is going to perform wonders among them, after which Pharaoh will let Israel go (3:20).

5:3   Moses replies by restating his request and warning of the inadvisability of defying the will of God.

5:4-18   Pharaoh does not take Moses or his request seriously. His response is to make Israel work harder, attempting to sap their energy and crush their spirit, so that they are too demoralised to press their case or cause any more trouble.

5:19-21   The response of Israel is to blame Moses and Aaron. Gone is the confidence of 4:29-31. We will find that this is typical of Israel's response to trouble or difficulty; they turn on the messenger.

5:22-23   Moses takes his troubles to God and mediates for the people.

6:1-5   God reassures Moses that everything is under control. He has remembered his covenant and will do what he has promised. Moreover, he is going to reveal himself in a way previously unknown. Abraham, Isaac and Jacob knew God as 'El Shaddai', God Almighty, but now his people will know him by his name YAHWEH (always written in the OT as the LORD).

6:6-8   In these verses God defines his name Yahweh. He does not explain what the word means, but rather tells Moses what he will do. It is these actions that will define his name forever.

These verses are given in a symmetrical form, which underlines their importance.

♦ I am the LORD.

♦ I will bring you out from under the yoke of the Egyptians. I will free you from being slaves to them.

♦ I will redeem you with an outstretched arm and with mighty acts of judgment.

♦ I will take you as my own people, and I will be your God.

♦ Then you will know that I am the LORD your God, who brought you out from under the yoke of the Egyptians. And I will bring you to the land I swore with uplifted hand to give to Abraham, to Isaac and to Jacob. I will give it to you as a possession.

♦ I am the LORD.

There are essentially 6 statements. Statements 1 and 6 say, 'I am the LORD.' Statements 2 and 5 say that God will bring them out from Egypt and from slavery. The core statements 3 and 4 speak of God taking them as his own people. He redeems them with an outstretched arm and mighty acts of judgment. These 2 strands of God's

25

personality, the one who redeems and judges, have been seen already in the events of the Flood. They will be seen in the story of the Exodus and are seen most clearly in the cross.

6:9   Moses shares this with the Israelites, but their minds are focussed on their troubles and they will not listen.

7:1-5   Because of Pharaoh's hardness of heart, God will multiply the signs and wonders he will do in Egypt. This will not only have the effect of freeing Israel, but also will make God known to the Egyptians.

7:8-13   Moses' signs do not impress Pharaoh. His magicians can do the same. We are told that Pharaoh's heart is becoming harder.

The Plagues

There are 9 plagues before the final plague on the firstborn and they come in 3 groups of 3. Each group starts with a command to Moses to get up early in the morning and go to confront Pharaoh (7:15, 8:20, 9:13). Each time God tells Pharaoh what the plagues will teach him about God.

7:17   'By this you will know that I am the LORD.'

8:22-23   God will deal differently with his people and make a distinction between his people and Pharaoh's people.

9:14   'So you may know that there is no-one like me in all the earth.'

The plagues in each set of three reflect these 'lesson aims'.

In all of this there is a battle going on for the possession of the Israelites. Do they belong to Pharaoh? (Pharaoh thinks so.) Or do they belong to the LORD? Through these plagues God is saying to Pharaoh:

- I am more powerful than you (and your gods).
- Israel are my people, not yours.
- I am in control of the situation, not you.

Pharaoh's heart is hard and God makes it harder (7:13,22; 8:15,32; 9:7,12,35; 10:16,20,27).

People around Pharaoh can see that it is useless to resist the will of God - the magicians (8:19), officials who feared the Lord protected their livestock (9:20), Pharaoh's officials said to let the Israelites go, because Egypt is ruined (10:7).

Many times Pharaoh asks for the plague to be taken away, appearing to relent, but then changes his mind, e.g. 8:8; 8:25f; 9:27. This is just as God said to Moses in 3:19, 'the king of Egypt will not let you go unless a mighty hand compels him.' The compelling act is the final plague, the death of the firstborn, after which Israel is bundled out of Egypt with great possessions, as foretold in Genesis 15:13-14. This is God's punishment on Pharaoh and Egypt for their treatment of God's firstborn, Israel, (Exodus 4:22). We will study this event in greater depth in the next study.

Lesson Summary

Pharaoh and the LORD are fighting for possession of the Israelites. God sends the plagues to show that he is in control, not Pharaoh, and the Israelites do not belong to Pharaoh, they are God's people. Through these events both Egyptians and Israelites see God's power and his care for his people. It seems that only Pharaoh cannot see he is fighting a battle which he cannot win and even that is under God's control. God reveals himself to Moses as the LORD, the God who has taken the Israelites as his people, who will rescue them from slavery with mighty acts of judgment and will take them to the land promised to their forefathers.

FOCUS ACTIVITY

Tug of War

Using a long rope, pole or stick, ask 2 group members to compete against each other. Draw a line on the floor between them, using masking tape or chalk, and ask each competitor to hold the end of the rope and take the strain. On the command to start, the first one to pull the other over the line is the winner. Run a competition to see who is the strongest group member. Finally choose a large leader and small group member to compete against each other. The leader has far more power than the group member. (If the leader is able to pull the strongest group member over the line easily, the point is made more clearly.)

In today's Bible study we will see that even someone as powerful as Pharaoh is no match for God.

Lesson Plan

1. Focus activity.

2. Write down on a board or piece of paper the letters, C E F F B A E and see if your group can guess what they stand for. (Creation, Eden, Fall, Flood, Babel, Abraham, Egypt.) If they need a clue, draw a line between B and A and write, 'new start'. Once they have guessed correctly, add a letter P and ask what comes next. (It could be Pharaoh or Plagues.)

3. There is a lot of information in this study, so you must decide how much depth and detail is appropriate for your group. In teaching it try to stick to the big themes: a) the battle for ownership of God's people, and b) God revealing himself to the Israelites and also to the Egyptians.

   The battle for ownership of God's people, set up by Pharaoh's statement in 5:2, is exciting and easy to grasp. Make a boxing poster titled, 'The Big Fight', with speech bubbles for God and

Pharaoh. Read 3:10,19-20 and 5:2 and use them to fill in the speech bubbles. You can then follow the course of the fight.

5:4-9	How does Pharaoh respond to Moses request?
5:19-21	How do the Israelites respond?
5:22-23	How does Moses respond?
6:1-8	How does God answer?

What were the 'mighty acts of judgment' God used to rescue his people from Egypt? See what they remember about the plagues. You can use pictures or letters as prompts. Do not spend too long on this or get bogged down in the precise details of the plagues; their purpose is much more important.

God revealing himself to the Israelites and also to the Egyptians. Follow what happens to Moses, Pharaoh, the Israelites and the Egyptians during the plagues. See if their attitudes change. Record what they learn about God. This can be done either as a whole group activity or in small groups with a feedback session. Make a chart to record who learns what. You will need to provide the group(s) with a list of references to work through. Choose your passages carefully.

4. Summarise what has been learned. Who is winning the big fight? Why is that important to Israel? What does it tell them about their God? How is God keeping his covenant blessing to the nations?

The covenant with Abraham included the promise that all nations would be blessed through him and his descendants. Although this is resulting in plagues for them at present, God is revealing himself also to Egypt and we can see some Egyptians responding to this revelation. In the next study we will see this more clearly, when some Egyptians leave Egypt and join with the Israelites.

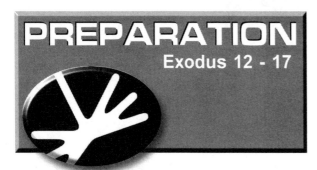

PREPARATION
Exodus 12 - 17

LESSON AIMS

To see God in action as judge, rescuer and redeemer and to understand the importance of remembering his deeds.

This passage is full of instructions, some are instructions for then and some for the future. Sandwiched between all these instructions are the remarkable events of God's rescue of his people from Egypt. The events in these chapters will be very familiar to most of the group, but the emphasis placed on remembering these events may not be. In the writer's mind, remembering these events in the future seems as important as the events themselves. Why?

The events are of crucial importance because they reveal the nature of God. They are God's revelation of himself. In 6:6-8 God defines himself through his name, the LORD, as the one who rescues his people, redeeming them from slavery and taking them to the place he has promised to give to them. Also he is the God who, with a mighty hand, judges those who defy him. The Exodus events show us this God of Mercy and Justice, whose character is consistent throughout Old and New Testaments.

Structure of the passage

12:1-2   This signifies a new start for the nation of Israel. Remembering God's character through these events is to be right at the heart of national life. God's people are to be 'those who remember'.

12:1-13   God instructs Moses about the present, how they are to escape his plague on the firstborn sons and male animals.

12:14-20   God instructs Moses about the future, how they are to celebrate the Feast of Unleavened Bread.

12:21-23   Moses instructs the people concerning the Passover arrangements for the present.

12:24-28   Moses instructs the people concerning the Passover arrangements for the future.

12:29-42   Narrative concerning the Passover and the flight from Egypt.

12:43-49   God instructs Moses about the future regulations for Passover celebration.

12:50-51   The people obey.

13:1-2   God instructs Moses about the consecration of the firstborn.

13:3-10   Moses instructs the people concerning the future celebration of the feast of Unleavened Bread.

13:11-16   Moses instructs the people concerning the future consecration of the firstborn.

13:17-31   Narrative concerning the crossing of the Red Sea.

15:1-21   The song of Moses and Miriam.

15:22-27   God's care for Israel - providing water.

16:1-36   God's care for Israel - providing food.

17:8-16   God's care for Israel - giving victory.

Instructions for the Passover

1. What to do now.

The instructions for the Passover meal are very specific. There are instructions regarding the quality of the animal, quantity of meat and manner of eating the meal. The blood of the animal daubed on the door frames was necessary to keep the family inside safe. 12:13 implies that Israelite families, who did not do this, would not be spared. Being ethnically Hebrew would not protect them. God's people are the ones who obey him.

Why the firstborn sons? God calls descendants of Israel his 'firstborn son'. In 4:22 God warns that, if Pharaoh will not release his 'firstborn', God will kill Pharaoh's firstborn son. This judgment on Pharaoh is felt in every family in the land who do not protect themselves with the blood of a lamb. As the ruler of the nation, all are his firstborn sons.

2. What to do in the future (12:43-49).

When the Israelites enter the land, the Passover will be celebrated as an annual event on the 10th day of the first month (12:1-2). Children are to be taught the significance of the celebration, so that the knowledge of God and his mercy is passed down to the next generation and will never be forgotten (12:24-27).

Who can celebrate it? Honorary members of the family, if circumcised, may celebrate the Passover. Aliens, who are circumcised and count themselves in with Israel, may celebrate it. Those, who are Israelites but uncircumcised, may **not** participate. This is a family celebration for those who are actively God's people, whether native born Israelites or those who have chosen to follow Israel's God.

The Feast of Unleavened Bread

This is to be celebrated following the Passover, between the 14th and 21st days of the month. It comes with the same instructions and warnings as the Passover. It will remind the Israelites of the coming out from Egypt. The narrative is full of references to the bread they carried out.

The Consecration of the Firstborn

Again, this is celebrated annually (13:10) and is an acknowledgement that the firstborn males of all families and all livestock belong to the LORD. This is a visual aid for the nation, reminding them that they are God's firstborn son. They belong to him.

These three annual events are to remind the Israelites of God's rescue and, therefore, of God's character (see 6:6-8). The Passover reminds them that he is the God who redeems his people 'with an outstretched arm and mighty acts of judgment'. God has shown them mercy. The Feast of Unleavened Bread reminds them that he is the God who 'brought them out from the yoke of the Egyptians'. They no longer belong in Egypt. The Consecration of the Firstborn reminds them that God has taken them as his people. They are God's possession. In all three there is an emphasis on teaching the next generation (12:24-27; 13:7-10; 13:14-16). Also there are warnings for those who do not comply (12:15,19,48-49).

The Exodus

These events are very familiar, however, some points are worth a special mention.

a) God always keeps his promises. What he says will happen, happens.

b) Pharaoh is thoroughly beaten. (Look back to his confidence in 5:2.) God has beaten Pharaoh in the battle for his people. The plundering of Egypt fulfils the promise in Genesis 15:14, but, more importantly, is the sign that God has won. These are the spoils of war.

c) The description of the Exodus in 12:31-39 draws attention to the dough that the Israelites took with them and why it contained no yeast. This paves the way for remembering the feast of Unleavened Bread.

d) Among the people fleeing from Egypt are non-Hebrews (12:37-38), who have joined up with God's people and their God.

Crossing the Red Sea and life in the Desert

Again, these stories are well known, but there are a few things to note.

a) Joseph's faith in God's promises was justified (Genesis 50:24-25, Exodus 13:19).

b) Almost certainly it was the Reed Sea and not the Red Sea that they crossed.

c) God's people are weak. Repeatedly, whenever there is difficulty, they take their eyes off God and turn on Moses their leader (14:10-12; 15:24; 16:2-3,20; 17:1-2,11). They have not changed really since 5:21.

d) Despite this, God continues to care for them (13:21-22; 14:29-30; 15:25; 16:4).

e) Moses' leadership is remarkably steady. He acts as mediator between the people and God. He asks God what to do and then encourages the people to trust in their God (14:13-14; 15:25).

f) God's victory over Pharaoh brings him glory and the Egyptians the knowledge of God (14:18,31). Even in judgment God brings blessing through Abraham's descendants.

g) Remembering is still in view (16:32-35; 17:14-16).

God's People

We are getting a clearer picture that God's people, though mostly physical descendants of Abraham, are starting to include those from other nations who want to serve the God of Israel. Also, Israelites who do not obey God's instructions are cut off from God's people. This is what we find in Galatians 3:6-9.

God's Place

The Land promised to God's people is getting closer. They are on their way at last and the instructions given for the festivals (12:43-49; 13:11) assume they will be living in their own land very soon. Nothing can stand in their way, not Pharaoh, not the Red Sea nor the Amalekites. Moses, in his song, talks about the people being guided to God's holy dwelling, God's sanctuary forever (15:13-18). He seems to have the restoration of 'Eden' in mind.

Under God's Authority

Clearly this is part of the package. Those who do not obey God are not part of his people.

Lesson Summary

The Exodus events reveal the very nature of God; they are God's revelation of himself. They must be remembered if God's nature is to be remembered accurately by his people from one generation to the next. He is the God who redeems his people with mighty acts of judgment and mercy. He rescues them and makes them his treasured possession. But we are starting to get the idea that God's people are not defined by their blood relationship to Abraham. God's people are the ones who obey him, including those who fear the LORD from other nations.

FOCUS ACTIVITY

Stuck in Slavery

Run a game of tag. One person is 'It' and the rest are Israelites. Anyone who is tagged must freeze with arms outstretched. They remain stuck in slavery until another group member runs under their arms to free them. Anyone who has been tagged and 'enslaved' 3 times is out of the game. The winner is the one who remains in the longest.

Today's story shows a dramatic and powerful rescue of God's people, who, like us in the game, could not rescue themselves.

Lesson Plan

1. Focus activity.

2. Get the group members one by one to mime a plague while the others guess which one. Ask the following questions.

   What was the purpose of the plagues? (*God revealing himself to Pharaoh and the Israelites as a sovereign God, who is more powerful than Pharaoh.*)

   What was God doing? (*Declaring ownership of his people and judging their captors.*)

   Can you remember what happened to Pharaoh, to his officials and to God's people as they experienced the plagues?

3. If possible, photocopy Exodus chapters 12-14 and spread it out on the table. Get your group to underline in colour the narrative passages, including present instructions for the Passover. You can divide the passage into sections and give each small group a section each.

   Get small groups (2 or 3 people) to research one or two of the following questions, using just the underlined passages.

   ◆ What do we learn about God's character?

   ◆ What do we learn about God's people?

   ◆ What effect did all this have on the Egyptians?

   ◆ What do we learn about Moses and his leadership?

   ◆ How does God demonstrate his care for his people?

   Feedback to the whole group, making sure that the important things are mentioned. The 'God's People / God's Place / God's Authority' structure may be helpful as you summarise.

4. Get the group to turn on to chapters 15-17 and pick out the main events. What do these add to our understanding of what God is like and what the people are like? What do they think of Moses and his leadership?

5. Go back to the underlined sheets. Point out that the rest of the passage is about remembering the Exodus events. Get different groups to find out about the three different festivals and report back. Make sure that they understand why remembering these events was crucial for the newly founded nation of Israel. Go back to the 5 questions in point 3 and see if these festivals add any further information (e.g. the forgetfulness of the people and God's provision for them).

6. Make the link to Jesus. In the New Testament Jesus is described as 'our Passover lamb' (1 Corinthians 5:7). Why does Paul describe him like that? How is Jesus like the Passover lamb? How is he different?

7. Today Jewish families still remember the events of the Passover, as instructed in Exodus. At what times do we remember Jesus and what he has done for us? (E.g. the Lord's supper, Christmas, Easter, baptisms.) Is this enough to help us to remember?

PREPARATION
Exodus 19 - 20; 24; 32 - 34

LESSON AIMS

To understand God's plan for his people in the world and the need for a mediator.

We have seen that God's purpose for his people was to take them out of Egypt, where they were slaves, and bring them into the land he had promised, where they would be able to serve him properly. Moses' song in 15:13-18 describes the land as God's dwelling place, his sanctuary. But how can God live with them in the land? If God could not have Adam and Eve living with him in the garden because of their sin, how will he be able to have sinful Israelites living with him in the land? The Israelites are sinners. We have seen them rebel against God many times. In the next 3 studies we will look at the covenant God makes with Moses and his people and the instructions God gives them for living as God's people. How they should behave towards God and other people and how to organise things so that, despite their sin, a holy God can live amongst them.

Throughout the Bible the covenant God makes with his people at Mount Sinai is seen as the foundation of his relationship with Israel. The key verses of this passage are 19:5-6 - 'Now if you obey me fully and keep my covenant, then out of all nations you will be my treasured possession. Although the whole earth is mine, you will be for me a kingdom of priests and a holy nation.' (Note how similar this is to the memory verse for weeks 6-12 from 1 Peter 2:9.)

19:1-2   This is the same mountain where Moses first encountered God at the burning bush. God said in 3:12 that, after he had rescued his people from Egypt, they would worship him on the mountain and here they are! However, they do not yet know how to worship God, what worshipping means and what kind of worship will be acceptable to him.

19:4-6   These are the key verses of this passage and in them we learn God's intention for his people. By obedience to his commands, God wants his people to be a 'kingdom of priests'. The role of a priest is to mediate between God and other people. They will be the means by which God is revealed to the world. Although what went on in the Tabernacle, and later

in the temple, is described as worship, there is another dimension to the worship God expects of them. They must obey God and live as a holy nation.

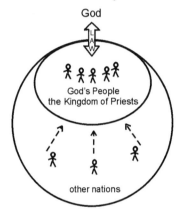

Obedience to God's commands does not create a relationship between God and his people, they are already God's redeemed people. But the commands tell them how to respond to their relationship with God and live within it. As with Noah, God establishes the relationship by grace and then instructs his people in what it means to live in righteousness. As they do this they will not only be blessed by their position of privilege before God, but also they will fulfil his purpose for them. This will draw other nations towards the one, true God.

19:7-8   The people respond positively to these 'terms and conditions'.

19:9   God will appear in a dense cloud and be heard talking to Moses, so that the people will put their trust in Moses, who has a special role in being the mediator between God and his people.

19:10-15 This underlines the importance of what comes next.

19:16-19 Encountering God, even in the form of a cloud, was a terrifying experience for the Israelites (see also 20:18-21).

19:20-25 This is about who can and cannot come up the mountain and how far. Nobody can come near unless God invites them (19:12-13,21,23-24) The priests are allowed part way up and they must consecrate themselves. Only Moses is allowed to go to the top of the mountain.

Despite being God's holy nation they cannot have full access to God and all access to God is on his terms. This differs from the pre-Fall situation when Adam could walk with God comfortably.

20:1-17 In the 10 commandments God tells them how they are to behave towards him (nos. 1-4) and towards each other (nos. 5-10). Note that the Israelites are not given the opportunity to discuss ways in which they can worship God. They are told by God what to do. The instructions for building the tabernacle and the sacrificial system follow the same pattern. God tells them exactly what he wants. Access to God is on his terms only.

20:18-21 The people respond. They want Moses to speak to them rather than God directly, or they fear they will die.

20:22-26 Makes it clear that manufacturing silver or gold images is unacceptable.

20:22-24:2 These chapters show how the 10 commandments are to be worked out in particular situations. In them we see God's particular concern for the vulnerable and the outsiders. We see also God's concern that his people should not behave like the surrounding nations.

24:4-11 Describes the sealing of the covenant.

24:8 These words seal God's covenant. Jesus uses these words at the Last Supper to describe how his blood will seal the New Covenant.

24:9-11 These verses are interesting. Perhaps they are a hint of what the covenant will ultimately bring - access to God.

24:12-13 Moses goes up the mountain again to receive instructions for the tabernacle.

32:1-6 While Moses is away we have the incident of the Golden Calf. It is completely clear from chapter 20 that this will not be acceptable to God. It seems to have been precipitated by boredom and shows great lack of judgment by Aaron. He seems to fear the people rather than God (32:22-23). This is a big problem and amounts to the people's rejection of God's authority over them. They deliberately ignore the rules God has given. They think there is some room for manoeuvre

within God's law. It is the sin of Eden repeated. What will God do?

The consequences

32:7-10 God knows exactly what they have done and his anger burns against them. The implication is that he will destroy his people and will make Moses into a great nation, fulfilling his promises to Abraham through Moses alone.

32:11-13 Moses pleads for the people, reminding God of his promises to Abraham, Isaac and Jacob and not wishing that God is dishonoured in the eyes of the Egyptians.

32:14 God relents. However, there is still judgment.

32:25-28 Slaughter of the revellers by the Levites.

32:35 A plague sent by God.

33:1-6 Now God will not go with them to the land.

33:12-17 Again Moses pleads with God.

33:12-13 Moses has found favour with God, but wants God to remember that the whole nation is his people.

33:14 God's answer is that Moses will know God's presence and be the recipient of his promise of 'Rest'.

33:15-16 Moses will not allow himself to be singled out from the fate of the whole nation. He insists that God's presence is necessary if they are to be distinctive among the other nations.

33:17 Moses wins another chance for God's people.

33:18-23 Moses asks to see God's glory. This is similar to the request to know God's name at the burning bush and also in v.13 and reflects a desire to know God more. However, this is not a request that God can grant. Despite being his chosen mediator, Moses is still a sinful man and could not survive a meeting with God face to face. What he gets is as much revelation of God's glory as is safe for him to receive and fresh revelation about God's name, concerning his compassionate acts of mercy which he has just displayed in his willingness to give Israel another chance.

34:1-35 God renews the covenant with more stone tablets. However, the covenant language is different this time. Instead of the covenant being made between God and his people it is made with Moses. God describes the people as Moses' people, not God's (34:10). Now the covenant can only be accessed by the people through a mediator.

Lesson Summary

God's intention for his people was for them to live in relationship with him, under his authority and receiving his blessing. This would speak to the surrounding nations of Israel's God and draw them towards worshipping him. God tells them through the commandments (and the chapters on their outworking) how they should behave as God's holy nation. While Moses is away getting further instructions from God, the people, aided by Aaron, deliberately do what has been forbidden, thereby breaking their covenant with God. Moses pleads for God to have mercy on them and God reforms the covenant, but this time with Moses as mediator.

the team's answers to the chief (one of the leaders). Only 1 person from each team is worthy to speak to the chief. Play a game of pictionary. Prepare a list of words on the theme of God's plan that have come into previous studies, e.g. law, bush, desert, sandals, etc. The spokesperson comes to the chief for the word, which they must draw for their team. No words or gestures can be used. Any member of the team can guess the word, but only the spokesperson can go to the chief with the answer. On return with the next word, the spokesperson whispers it to another group member, who draws it for the team to guess. (The spokesperson, knowing the answer, must refrain from 'guessing'!) Continue until all the words have been used. The first team to correctly guess all the words is the winner. In today's Bible study we will see how God spoke to his people through a spokesperson, or mediator.

1. Focus activity.

2. Ask the group members to recount a past event that they will always remember and why. It could be memorable because it was pleasant or unpleasant. Ask them to think of something that they ought to remember but do not. Why is it difficult to remember?

   Lead in to what the Israelites were to remember, (the Exodus events through celebrating the festivals), and why it was so important, (the character of God was being revealed). Do they think that they would ever be in danger of forgetting these events and therefore forgetting what God was like? Briefly discuss.

3. God, having brought his people out of Egypt, he instructs them how to live as his people and what his purpose is for them.

   a) **God's purpose for them**

   Study 19:1-6, drawing attention to the significance of the location and what God said they would do there. Consider what God meant by his promises in 19:4-6 and how that will fit in with God's purposes for the whole world (the diagram may be useful here - see page 31).

   b) **How to live as God's people**

   See how many of God's commandments your group can remember. Look at 20:1-17 and fill in the gaps. Tell them that chapters 21-23 give examples of how these principles work out in a variety of everyday situations.

   Read 19:10-19. How does God convey that what he has to say should be taken seriously?

   Read 20:18-20. How do the people respond? Why does God want them to be frightened?

4. Read 20:22-23 to lead into a recap of the Golden Calf story (which they should remember). What will God do about this rebellion? What will Moses do?

   To answer these 2 questions, get 3 small groups to read 32:7-14; 32:19-30 and 32:35 - 33:4,12-17 and feedback to the group.

5. Read 33:19-23. What does Moses learn about God? How has this been demonstrated in God's actions?

6. Use a diagram or flash cards to summarise how the covenant was made and then broken, how Moses came between God and his people to plead for them, and that the covenant is now re-established with Moses as mediator.

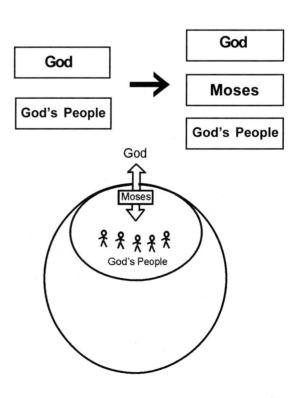

PREPARATION

Exodus 25 - 31;
35 - 40

LESSON AIMS

To understand the difficulties of God living with his people.

God's plan was for his chosen people to live in fellowship with him and obey his law. As they did this God would bless them. This blessing in relationship with God would demonstrate to other nations what God is like and draw them towards worshipping the one true God. However, there is a problem with all this, the problem of sin. As we have already seen, sin stops the people obeying God's law and remaining distinctive and blessed. But there is another problem. In Exodus 20:19 the people say, 'Do not have God speak to us or we will die.' Their instincts are correct. God cannot live with sinful people - even Moses (33:21-23). The last time God lived with his people was in the Garden of Eden and their sin resulted in them being driven out. How then can a holy God promise to live amongst sinful people?

The next two studies are about the instructions God gave to make this possible. This lesson is about the Tabernacle - a sanctuary where God could 'dwell' among his people.

Exodus 25-31 contain the instructions given by God to Moses concerning the construction of the tabernacle, its furnishings and the clothing of the priests. Exodus 35-40 covers the same ground as chapters 25-31, but this time the instructions are being followed. All the instructions from God are very precise. The repetition in chapters 35-40 tells us that they were carried out exactly as God commanded.

25:1-7   The materials for the tabernacle were to be a freewill gift from the Israelites.

25:8   God was promising to dwell among them. This was a big promise, a promise to do something he had not done since Adam and Eve's expulsion from the garden of Eden.

25:9   The tabernacle had to be made exactly as God showed Moses. This was not just a test of obedience for the Israelites, but also the Tabernacle had to be a suitable place for God. Hebrews 8-10, in describing Jesus' work of atonement, describe the tabernacle as being a 'copy' of the sanctuary in heaven (clearest in Hebrews 8:5).

36:1   The work starts under the direction of two capable project managers. It is to be done 'just as the LORD has commanded'.

36:3b-5   It was important to stop the people bringing more gifts than were necessary. The Tabernacle must be made exactly according to God's instructions - it must not be grander, larger or more ornate than God's plans state.

(See Page 37 for plan of the Tabernacle and Courtyard)

Basically the tabernacle was a portable sanctuary for God to dwell in. Around the outside was a courtyard. The tabernacle is also called the Tent of Meeting, which is not to be confused with Moses' private tent outside the camp (33:7-11). The 'meeting' which takes place is the meeting of people with God. The tabernacle could be dismantled, moved and set up in another place. All the furnishings had poles, so that they could be picked up easily and carried without being touched.

36:8-38   The tabernacle was a box-like structure made of wooden frames set in silver bases, covered with a tent made of goats' hair. Over this were 2 further coverings, one of rams' skins and one of sea cow hides. It was anchored with ropes and pegs. The tabernacle was divided by a curtain into an inner and an outer room. The outer room was called the Holy Place and the inner room the Most Holy Place, or the Holy of Holies. It was in this inner room that God would be present in a special way.

37:1-9   The only piece of furniture in this inner room was the Ark of the Covenant (see diagram on page 38). This was a wooden chest overlaid with gold and was 'centre stage' in the tabernacle. All dimensions are given in cubits. A cubit is the distance between the elbow and the tip of the middle finger, so the Ark would be very roughly 140 x 80 x 80 cm, which is not very big for such an important item. Inside were kept the stone tablets on which were written the commandments, which emphasised God's rule over his people by his word. Later, Aaron's staff which budded and the jar of manna were also kept inside the Ark.

The lid of the Ark, called the Atonement Cover, was made of a single piece of pure gold. A cherub was fashioned at each end, with wings spread upwards, overshadowing the cover. God would meet with Moses between these 2 cherubim. This atonement cover became thought of as the throne of God. It is also called the Mercy Seat.

36:35-36 The dividing curtain was intricately woven to a God-given desgin. It had cherubim worked into it, reminding the people of the cherubim who were set at the entrance to the Garden of Eden to prevent Adam and Eve returning (Genesis 3:24). It reminded people that they could not come into the presence of God.

The Holy Place had three pieces of furniture (see diagrams on page 39).

37:10-16 The table contained 12 loaves of bread, one for each of the tribes of Israel. The priests replaced the bread once a week, eating the old loaves as a meal in God's presence (Leviticus 24:5-9).

37:17-24 The lampstand was kept burning continuously (Leviticus 24:1-4).

37:25-28 The altar of incense. The priest offered incense twice a day from this altar as a symbol of the people's prayers (Luke 1:8-10).

All the tabernacle furnishings and utensils were made of gold, or overlaid with gold, which emphasised how special this place was.

38:9-20 The courtyard. The tabernacle was surrounded by a large courtyard, within which most of the everyday work of the priests took place, including the sacrifices. The walls of the coutyard were made of linen cutains, supported by wooden poles set into bronze bases and anchored with ropes and pegs.

38:1-8 Within the courtyard was a bronze basin and the altar of burnt offering, which was a large square structure made of wood covered with bronze (see diagram on page 39). All the utensils used with this altar were made of bronze also. It was placed close to the courtyard curtain, so would be the first thing anyone would see on entry.

The bronze basin (see diagram on page 39) was placed between the altar of burnt offering and the tabernacle and was used by the priests to wash their hands and feet to purify themseves before entering the tabernacle.

Ordinary Israelites were allowed to enter the tabernacle courtyard when bringing an offering. Only priests were allowed access into the tabernacle to tend the lampstand, offer incense, etc. No-one was allowed to enter the Holy of Holies, except the High Priest once a year on the Day of Atonement (covered in the next lesson).

The tabernacle was to be placed in the middle of the camp, where the tent of the prince or ruler would be in a normal nomadic community. Chapter 40 states how Moses set up everything they had made in the places where God had instructed them to be.

40:33 It was finished. Now the big question was, would God accept it? Had they made it accurately enough? Had any human 'adaptation' entered into the design, making it unfit for him? It's a tense moment.

40:34-35 God's glory, that terrifying presence on the mountain (20:18-19), moved towards the camp and filled the tabernacle. It was a big moment - now God was dwelling with his people as their Lord.

40:36-38 This gives us an idea of how things worked as God led his people. God's presence was constantly visible to the Israelites during this period of their history.

So is this now Eden restored? Can God and his people now live side by side? The answer is, of couse, NO! Although God is visibly dwelling with his people now, the tabernacle is a constant reminder that they are not really able to have fellowship with him. The tabernacle not only gets more special and grand as you get further towards the place where God's glory is, but also gets more difficult and dangerous to enter. On entering the courtyard, the altar of burnt offering reminds of the need to atone for sin and the bronze basin of the need to be purified. The dividing curtain in the tabernacle was not only a physical barrier to the presence of God, but also had a warning embroidered into the fabric. In fact it was a huge 'no entry' sign, denying access to God. Even Moses could not enter the tabernacle once God's glory had filled it (40:35).

Lesson Summary

God gave Moses very detailed instructions for the construction of a portable sanctuary where God could be visibly present with his people. The people made it just as God had said and God's awesome presence moved from the mountain to fill the inner room of the tabernacle. On one hand God appeared to be living with his people, but on the other hand the whole design of the tabernacle reminded them that their sin made real access to God impossible.

Where do you live?

Cut out pictures of houses/castles/tents/living areas for famous people or animals from magazines and newspapers and stick them up around the room. The group members must try and work out who lives where. You might want to give them a list of the inhabitants for them to match up with the pictures. Some suggestions:

Buckingham Palace	-	the Queen
Wigwam	-	a Native American
Tent	-	a camper, such as a girl guide or boy scout
Nest	-	a bird
Burrow	-	a rabbit
Kennel	-	a dog
Caravan	-	a gypsy
Igloo	-	an Eskimo

Summarise the answers and point out how silly it would be for the Queen to live in a kennel, or for you to live in a nest. Where you live reflects who you are. In today's Bible study we will see where God chose to dwell with his people.

Lesson Plan

1. Focus activity.

2. Draw the diagram used in lesson 10, but leave it unlabelled (see below). Get the group to fill in the labels.

God

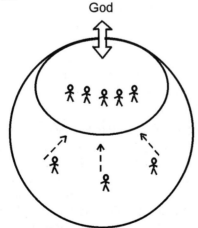

Recap on God's purposes for the nation - as they lived in relationship with God as a holy nation, God would be revealed to the surrounding nations.

Ask how God's people were going to maintain their distinctiveness (i.e. through the law) and whether that was going to be easy for them?

Show the picture of a golden calf (see page 38) and use this as a prompt for remembering how the Israelites have

a) rebelled against God's authority already (idols are not allowed).

b) are not being distinctive (golden calves were the kind of aids to worship that pagans used).

They have already broken God's covenant.

Show them the label with 'Moses' on it. Get the group to remember how Moses pleaded for the people and how the covenant was reformed with Moses as mediator. Insert the 'Moses' label between God and his people on the diagram.

3. The Tabernacle. Write down the word TABERNACLE and see what your group remembers about it.

4. Get the group to find how many chapters it took for God to give Moses the instructions for the tabernacle. Draw attention to the huge amount of detail in the passage and that the instructions must be followed exactly. Get the group, either individually or in pairs, to research one or more parts of the tabernacle or furnishings, giving them appropriate references.

    Tabernacle, altar of incense, lampstand, curtain, altar of burnt offering, ark of the covenant, courtyard, bronze basin.

    While they do this stick pictures of the tabernacle and its furnishings randomly on a wall or spread them out on the table. (These can be photocopied from pages 38-39.) See if the group members can recognise the item they have been reading about. One by one they can pick out their item and tell the group about it. The teacher can prompt or add information.

5. Read chapter 40:1-33 together and assemble the tabernacle as a group. Point out the increasing grandeur as you move towards the Holy of Holies and also the increasing restrictions on entry.

    Read Hebrews 8:1-5. What does this tell us about why God gave such precise instructions for the tabernacle?

6. The last time God lived with his people was in Eden. It was a big step for God to come and live amongst his people again. Lead into the reading of 40:34-38 by drawing attention to the suspense they would have felt.

    Point out the paradox of God coming to live among his people, but not even Moses being allowed in.

Plan of the Tabernacle and its Contents

(The Tabernacle is to scale with the courtyard. All the contents are double their size.)

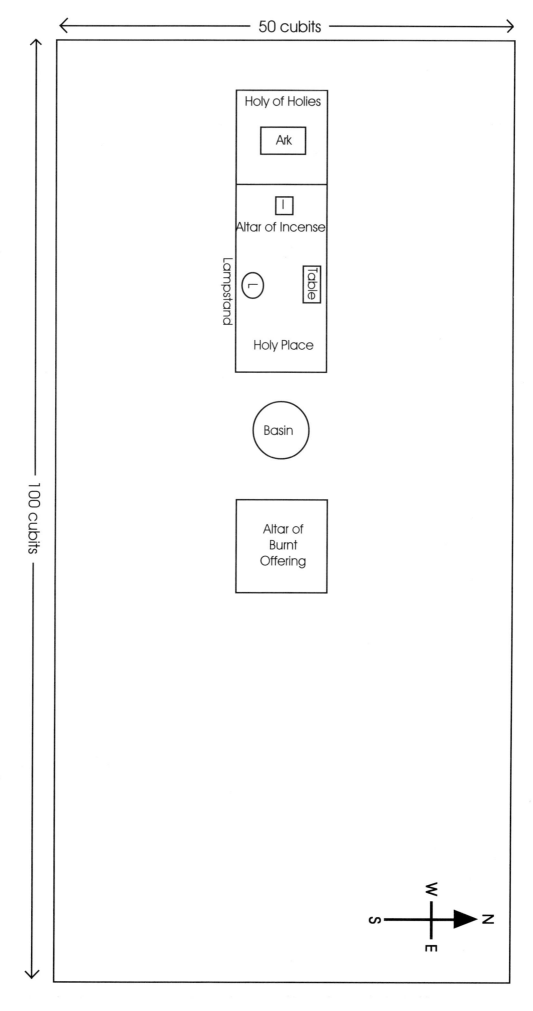

50 cubits

100 cubits

Holy of Holies

Ark

Altar of Incense

Lampstand

Table

L

Holy Place

Basin

Altar of
Burnt
Offering

W
S — N
E

Ark of the Covenant

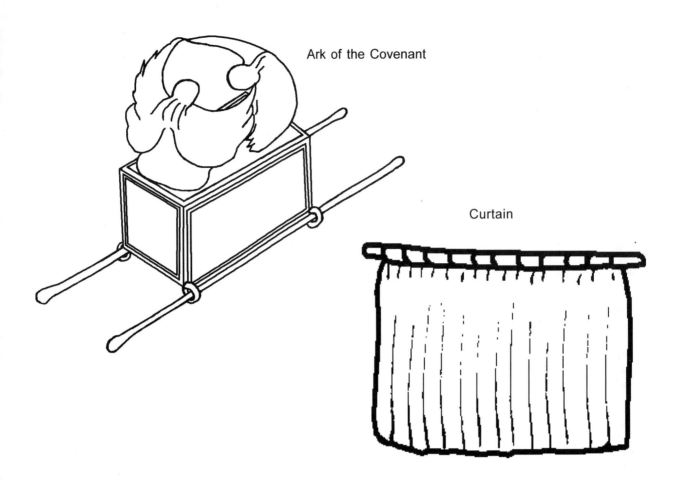

Curtain

Golden Calf

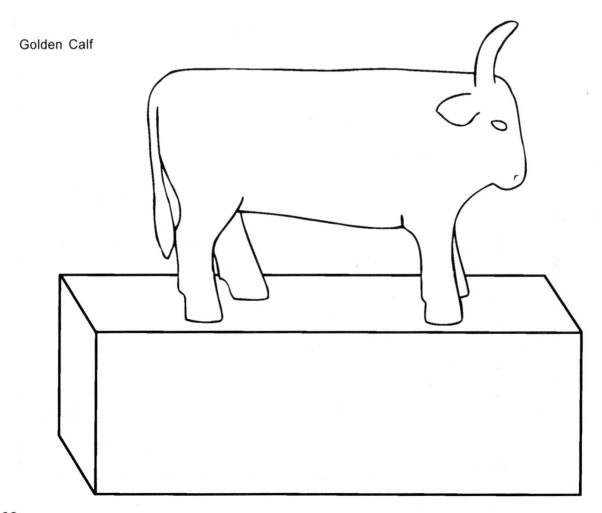

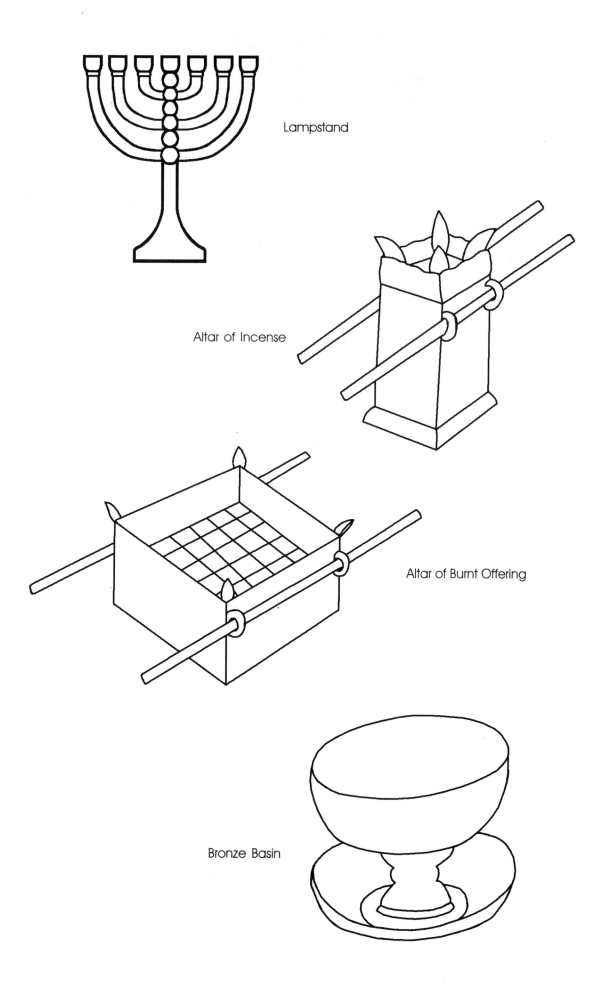

Lampstand

Altar of Incense

Altar of Burnt Offering

Bronze Basin

Week 12
Living as God's People
- the Sacrifices

PREPARATION
Leviticus 1 - 5; 16

LESSON AIMS
To understand that any encounter with God requires atonement for sin.

The tabernacle was not only a place for God to live, but also for sacrifices. Nearly all of these sacrifices involved the death of an animal. Most of us recoil from this idea and find it difficult to understand why this activity would be pleasing to God. However, it ought to remind us of what a huge problem sin is for anyone wanting to encounter God. We must not forget that our own relationship with God is only possible because of the shedding of the blood of Christ 2000 years ago. The animal was to be brought by the worshipper to the entrance of the tabernacle courtyard. Then he was to lay his hand on the animal's head, symbolising the transfer of the worshipper's guilt onto the animal. Next he had to slaughter the animal and its blood would be taken by the priest to be sprinkled on the altar. The animal's life was accepted instead of the worshipper's. In effect, the animal was dying in his place.

The detail of the instructions for sacrifices of different types varies. The gender and kind of animal required is specific to that sacrifice, as is exactly what must be done with each part of the animal. There are two important things to note:

1) As for the tabernacle, the instructions for the sacrifices were very detailed, reinforcing that all acceptable worship is on God's terms. Unauthorised worship is never a good idea (Leviticus 10:1-3).

2) The death of an animal was needed in any kind of encounter with God, not just as a sin offering. Atonement for sin was necessary before someone could even say thank you to God.

Leviticus 1-5 gives instructions for 3 main types of sacrifices:

1. Gift Sacrifices

♦ Burnt offerings. These were a way of saying thank you to God for some particular benefit the worshipper had received, or to ask for guidance on some issue. Sometimes they were just an expression of the worshipper's joy in being part of God's chosen people. In this sacrifice the whole animal was burnt.

♦ Grain Offerings. The first fruits of a crop were offered to thank God for a successful harvest.

2. Fellowship Offerings

These offerings were sometimes called Peace Offerings and were a way for the people to remember God's covenant relationship with them. Instead of the whole animal being burnt, only the animal's fat and inner parts were burnt on the altar, the rest being eaten in a fellowship meal. The Passover lamb was a fellowship offering.

3. Sacrifices for the Forgiveness of Sins

Sin Offerings and Guilt Offerings. These were a way of dealing with specific wrongdoing, but it is not clear which kind of sins required a guilt offering and which a sin offering. The sprinkling of blood was an important element of the sin offering. If it was brought by a member of the community, it only needed to be sprinkled on the altar of burnt offering. However, if it was brought by a priest the blood had to be sprinkled 7 times before the curtain in the Holy Place and also on the horns of the altar of incense.

The Day of Atonement (Leviticus 16)

Sin was all pervasive among the people of Israel. Even the constant sacrificing of animals could not keep the tabernacle from being polluted by the people's sin. If God was going to continue to live among them, once a year the High Priest had to carry out a special ceremony to purify it. This happened on the Day of Atonement.

16:29-31 The people had to prepare themselves for this day.

16:3-4 It was the job of Aaron and, after him, the High Priest (16:31-34).

Four animals were involved: a bull as a sin offering for the High Priest and his family, a ram as a burnt offering, a goat as a sin offering for the people and a goat to be the scapegoat.

16:13 The smoke from the incense prevented the priest from seeing the atonement cover. The verse suggests that, if he did, he would die. Therefore it was a very dangerous job and in NT times the High Priest entered the Holy of Holies with a rope tied around his ankles, so that, if he was struck dead, he could be hauled out without the need for another priest to enter.

16:16-19 Sprinkling the blood 7 times cleansed the Most Holy Place. Sprinkled blood also cleansed the other areas of the Tent of Meeting. It made atonement for the people, whatever their sins had been. It represented a kind of annual fresh start for God's people.

16:20-22 Both goats had the sins of the people confessed over them. Both demonstrated the effects of sin in different ways. The guilt transferred onto the sacrificed goat resulted in its death, whereas the guilt transferred onto the scapegoat resulted in its exile from the camp, never to return. Because of the goats, God's people need not die nor be driven out from God's presence.

Lesson Summary

Sin is a real problem. A sinful person cannot encounter God and survive. Through the sacrifices God provided a way whereby his anger at a person's sin could be deflected onto an animal substitute. This was the only way that anyone could draw near to God. God's problem with sin remains. In these days we still need God's anger to be turned aside if we are to encounter him. But, instead of bringing an animal sacrifice, we come to God trusting in the death of Jesus, the perfect sacrifice for all time. There is no other way of drawing near to God.

FOCUS ACTIVITY

The Preparation Game

The aim of the game is to use the 3 activities listed to guess the event about to happen. Suggestions are:

♦ key, ignition, handbrake - starting a car

♦ hot water, liquid, brush - washing up

♦ wash hands, sit down, pick up cutlery - eat a meal

♦ sit down, pick up pen, write name - sit an examination paper

♦ set a date, send out invitations, decorate a room - have a party.

Write the various lists of instructions on paper around the room. The group members, either individually or in pairs, must guess the activities about to happen.

Today we will see what preparations God's people had to make before they could meet with him.

Lesson Plan - see page 42

1.   Focus activity.

2.   Rebuild the tabernacle using the visual aids from last week. Make a cloud from a piece of cotton wool to signify the presence of God and ask what conditions would have to be fulfilled for God to be able to occupy the tabernacle? (*They would have to make it exactly as God said.*)
     What would have happened if people had made it grander than God had said? How did Moses ensure that this did not happen (36:3-5)?
     Get one of the group members to put the cloud in the right place. Now God can dwell with his people. But can he? What about sin?

3.   *Draw an outline of a person on one piece of paper and a crown with God written on it on another.* In Eden there was no problem - people and God could be together. *Place the pieces of paper side by side.*

Then sin came into the world. *Write 'sin' onto the person.*

Now God and people were enemies. Adam and Eve were banished from God's presence. *Remove the person page.*

If God and a sinful person came face to face what would happen? *Bring the papers together.* God's anger would burn against that person and they would be destroyed. *Screw up the person paper.* That presents a big problem for people and God living together. It would be very dangerous.

So God provided a way in which that anger could be deflected. *Have another piece of paper with a person on it, with a removable label saying 'sin' stuck on, and a third with an animal outline. Bring them together to 'God'.*

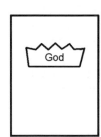  

As a person came to meet God he put his hand on the animal's head, which symbolised the passing of his sin onto the animal. *Swap the 'sin' label onto the animal.*

Then God's anger at the sin was deflected onto the animal, which was slaughtered immediately. *Screw up the animal paper.* So the sin was dealt with and the person could live.

This is the system God provided for dealing with the sin of his people, enabling him to live among them.

4. Look at one offering in detail. Leviticus 1:1-9 describes the burnt offering and is straightforward. Note particularly the detail of the instructions - the quality of the animal, the transfer of guilt, that the worshipper had to do the slaughtering himself, the importance of the sprinkling of blood.

5. Outline the different kinds of sacrifices, pointing out that all, except the grain offering, required the death of an animal. All encounters with God need to involve atonement.

6. Explain the need for the ritual purification of the Tent of Meeting on the Day of Atonement. Read Leviticus 16 and write a list of the events of the Day of Atonement in chronological order. What did the fate of the goats demonstrate to the people about God and sin?

7. Ask the group why we do not sacrifice animals anymore in our church services? Make sure that they understand that Jesus' death was the sacrifice for sin which turned aside God's anger. Like the animal, Jesus died in our place, but, unlike an animal, his death dealt with sin forever. Ask if there is any other way people will be safe from God's anger at their sin when they die? If there is time read Hebrews 10:11-22.

PREPARATION

Numbers 1 - 14, Deuteronomy 20; 28, Joshua 1 - 8

LESSON AIMS

To understand that Israel's experience of living in the land depends on their obedience to God.

We left the Israelites living in the desert. At the centre of their camp was the tabernacle, the place where God was present in a visible way. Everyone could see his presence, even if they were forbidden to approach him because of his holiness and their sin. Whereas other nomadic cultures had their prince living in the central tent, the Israelites had their God, who was their King and under whose authority they lived. When it was time for them to move on the cloud of God's glory would lift from the tabernacle and the Israelites would pack up the tabernacle and all their possessions and follow where God led. When the cloud stopped they would stop and set up camp once again.

It was not far from Mount Sinai to the Promised Land. The book of Numbers tells of the preparations made for the march, how the tribes were counted, unified and organised for the battles ahead (chapters 1-4) and how they purified themselves so as to be ready to take the land as the holy people of God (chapters 5-10). In no time at all they had reached the land of Canaan. Chapter 13 is a well-known story of what happens when 12 men are sent ahead to spy out the land.

13:1-2   This advance party is sent at God's command.

13:17-20 They are to explore the land thoroughly and bring back tokens to encourage the people with how good this land is.

13:23   The land was wonderfully fertile.

13:26-29 The spies confirm that the land is very good, but are frightened of the people who live there. Their fear has made them exaggerate the problems posed by the current inhabitants of Canaan. By verses 32-33 things have become ridiculous.

13:30   Caleb speaks as a man who has remembered that this is the land God has promised to them. Certainly they can take it. Will God's people follow the instructions of the God whose physical presence they can see living among them? He is the one who they saw defeat Pharaoh and the greatest world power of the day. He has rescued them, cared for them, fed them and has kept all his promises to date. Will they trust their God or will they believe in the judgment of men who say the land is full of giants?

14:1-4   The people wobble.

14:4-9   Moses tries to encourage them with faultless logic.

14:10   The people rebel.

14:11-12 God's patience is exhausted. God's inclination is to strike down all these disobedient people with plague and make a new nation through Moses. This is just what happened after the golden calf incident. Just as Moses pleaded for the people then, he pleads for them now, asking that God would not destroy them for the sake of his reputation among the surrounding nations.

14:20-24 God forgives the people, but vows that no-one who has experienced his mighty acts in Egypt and subsequently rebelled will see the Promised Land. God leads them back towards the Red Sea and for the next 40 years leads his complaining people round and round the desert until the Egypt generation have died out.

The census in chapter 26 signals a new generation of Israelites. From this point they are getting ready to enter the land once more. Deuteronomy 20 gives some instructions for war.

20:1-4   The most important quality they need to occupy the land successfully is faith in God and courage to do this, despite their natural fear. This will be more important than military prowess.

20:16-18 When they fight against those who are occupying the land God has promised them, all surviving people and livestock must be killed. If they are left alive they will contaminate the land and be the cause of the Israelites compromising in their worship of God. This seems harsh to us, but we need to understand that it was central to God's plan. God's people needed to occupy a 'clean' land if they were to fulfil their role of demonstrating God to the surrounding nations.

Deuteronomy 28 is very important. It takes place at the end of Moses' life when Joshua is about to succeed him as leader and the Israelites are in Moab getting ready to enter the land.

28:1-14   God will bless them wonderfully and in every way if they obey him. If they are willing to live under his authority they will enjoy prosperity (v.3-6), and victory over their enemies (v.7). They will fulfil the role God has for them amongst the nations (v.9-10), and they will always be at the top (v.13)! But they must obey God's commands exactly.

28:15-68   However, if they do not obey, curses will come upon them. This is a much longer list. There will be poverty, (v.16-19), disease and plague (v.21-22,59f), defeat by enemies (v.25-26), lawlessness (v.30), conquest and exile (v.36,49f,64). It is a fearsome list and reverses the promises made to Abraham. They will be a poor and humiliated nation, they will lose their land and their distinctiveness and be indistinguishable from other nations in their national and religious life.

During the rest of the Old Testament we see the outworking of these blessings and curses in the life of the nation. When Israel is obedient, blessing, victory and prosperity follows. When they turn away from God, they become poor, defeated and humiliated.

Joshua

1:1-9   God commends Joshua as his chosen successor to Moses. His job is going to be that of a military commander as he leads the people to take possession of their land. But God's instructions to him are not about military matters. They encourage him to put his trust firmly in the Lord and meditate on the Law of the Lord. Joshua is to hold tight to God and his Law.

    God will give them the land. Just as he brought them out of Egypt he will bring them into Canaan. He demonstrates this in their crossing the Jordan to enter the land.

3:9-17   This is deliberately reminiscent of the Red Sea crossing. God has opened the way.

God proves this again as he intervenes in the capture and destruction of the towns of Jericho and Ai.

8:30-35   Joshua proves himself a worthy successor to Moses, as he points the people towards their God at the covenant renewal ceremony held on Mount Ebal. This time, along with the burnt offerings and the reading of the Law, the blessings and curses are read aloud also. God is fulfilling his plan and giving them the land, but there are conditions attached.

Lesson Summary

Not long after God made the covenant with his people at Mount Sinai, they arrive at the border of the Promised Land. It is a beautiful, fertile land, 'flowing with milk and honey'. Although it has other occupants, God has promised it to his people. However, the Israelites can only see the potential difficulties of conquering the land and are not prepared to trust their God, despite having seen his power and experienced his care. Because of their unbelief, that generation experiences God's judgment and dies in the wilderness. Forty years later a new generation crosses the Jordan river and enters the land under the leadership of Joshua. As they fight they experience God giving them the land. But God has warned them through the blessings and curses that their success in this land will depend on their obedience to him.

Listen to the Captain

Nominate one person to be the captain. The captain calls out various instructions for the remaining group members to follow. The 4 sides of the room are designated Port, Starboard, Bow and Stern and, when these are called out the group members must run to the appropriate side of the room. Other actions to follow are:

♦ climb the rigging   - mime the action of climbing up a rope

♦ man the lifeboats   - piggyback with a partner

♦ Captain's coming   - salute

♦ Swab the decks   - mime mopping the floor

The last person to do the action or arrive at a place must hop for the remainder of the game. (The hoppers are not counted when deciding who is last.) The winner is the last person who is able to run.

If you obeyed orders quickly it was better, because you could run on both feet. Disobeying, or being slow to obey orders made the game more difficult, because you could only hop. Today we will see how much easier life was for God's people when they obeyed him.

Lesson Plan

1. Focus activity.

2. Write out, or type and enlarge, the defining statement about the LORD from Exodus 6:6-8.

   ♦ I am the LORD,

   ♦ I will bring you out from under the yoke of the Egyptians. I will free you from being slaves to them,

   ♦ I will redeem you with an outstretched arm and with mighty acts of judgment.

   ♦ I will take you as my own people, and I will be your God.

   ♦ Then you will know that I am the LORD your God, who brought you out from under the yoke of the Egyptians. And I will bring you to the land I swore with uplifted hand to give to Abraham, to Isaac and to Jacob. I will give it to you as a possession.

   ♦ I am the LORD.

   You could make more than one copy, cut it up into sentences and have a competition to see who can assemble it correctly first. This is probably best done in twos or threes, not individually.

   Use the statements about Yahweh to recap on the story of the Israelites so far. Pick them out as you talk about them.

   a) Use the slavery statements to remember how life was for the Israelites in Egypt and how we know God was still in charge (*increased birth rate, Moses rescued and called, God hearing and remembering his covenant with Abraham, Isaac and Jacob*).

   b) Use the outstretched arm and mighty acts of judgment to remember the showdown with Pharaoh, the Passover and the Exodus.

   c) Use 'you will be my people and I will be your God' to remember how the law showed them how to be God's people. Also, how God could live among them, despite their sin, because of the provision of the tabernacle and the sacrificial system.

   d) The promise of a land, which will lead into this study. Today they reach the land.

3. Describe how the Israelites organised and purified themselves for the last lap of their journey to the Promised Land. Using a map (see page 79), roughly show the route they would have taken, describing how the cloud would lift from the tabernacle to show them when and where to go.

4. Numbers 13 and 14. The story of the spies is very well-known. Write on a piece of paper headings for 3 columns: the spies said, Caleb said, the people said. Get the group to remember what happened when the spies returned, using the headings. Ask the group whom they think they would have believed?

   Write on another piece of paper: God said, Moses said, God said. Read 14:11-25 to get the answers.

   Read 14:25 and show on the map how they turned back towards the desert and wandered for 40 years.

5. When that generation had died out they prepared to enter the Promised Land again. Read Deuteronomy 20:1-4. What would they need to conquer the land? What did their fathers lack when they failed to enter it earlier?

   Explain the role of the blessings and curses from Deuteronomy 28. Divide into 3 groups and get 1 to write down the blessings and the other 2 to write down the curses, taking half the passage each. Why should they take these promises seriously? What would they have done if they were Israelites?

6. Get the group to remember how the Israelites crossed the Jordan, pointing out that this is the end of the journey started at the Red Sea, and how God gave victory at Jericho and Ai. If necessary remind them about God's command to destroy all the people and livestock in those cities and make sure that they understand why it was necessary.

7. Read the account of the renewal of the covenant on Mount Ebal (Joshua 8:30-35).

PREPARATION

Joshua 13:1-7; 21: 43-45; 23:1 -24:33, Judges 1 - 2

LESSON AIMS

To understand that the difficulties Israel faced in the promised land were result of disobedience.

In our first study in Genesis we saw that God rested on the 7th day, because creation was finished. What it means to live in God's rest was explored in the account of Adam and Eve's life in the Garden. It can be summarised as God's people, living in the place God has provided, under his authority and can be represented in this diagram.

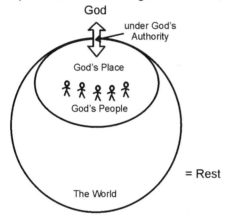

Since God made his covenant with Abraham, we have been waiting for God to bring about this rest again. In Psalm 95:8-11 the life in the land is described as God's rest. The disobedient Israelites died in the wilderness because God declared that they would not enter his 'rest'. Deuteronomy 8:7-9 describes what the promised land will be like, using Eden type language. Now that the land has been taken by the Israelites, will they enjoy 'rest'? Will it be an Eden experience? We know from last week's study that this will depend on whether they obey God fully and receive blessings, or turn away from him and receive curses.

The book of Joshua is full of battle accounts, of how God went before his people and gave them victory over the inhabitants of the land. There is no doubt that the land is being given to them by God. However, at the end of Joshua's life large areas still had to be conquered (Joshua 13:1). But surely God will give it to his people and drive out the current occupants (13:6). The whole of the Promised Land is given by God to the various tribes, even though they have yet to take possession of it (Joshua 13-21). At the end of this section, in 21:43-45 God gives them rest on every side. This is restated in 23:1. Like Moses, Joshua makes a farewell speech which is followed by a renewal of the covenant.

In chapter 23 Joshua speaks to the leaders.

1. Joshua reminds them of how they have seen God at work, fulfilling his promises, and how he has driven out many great and powerful nations. He tells them to persist with the conquest and God will give them the whole land as their own.

2. He urges them to be strong and obey God's instructions in the Book of the Law, to maintain their distinctiveness and not to associate with the pagan nations who live with them in the land.

3. He warns them that turning away from God's instructions will incur his wrath and result in them perishing from the land.

In chapter 24 Joshua speaks to the people.

1. He gives them a history lesson, reminding them of God's covenant and how he has proved his faithfulness to them time and time again.

2. He tells them to serve God exclusively and to get rid of any alternatives, or it will be disastrous for them.

3. He gives them a challenge and a lead.

24:15   'Choose for yourselves this day whom you will serve.' 'As for me and my household, we will serve the LORD.'

24:19-24   The covenant is renewed.

24:19-20   This is a very strong warning. God is jealous. This is not a negative attribute, but is a sign of his love and commitment to them. He will not put up with them worshipping other gods in addition to him anymore than a loving husband would share his wife with another man. If they turn away from him, God will curse them just as he will bless them if they obey him.

24:21-22   They answer, 'We will serve the LORD.'

24:23   This would suggest that already they had started to serve foreign gods. These had to be got rid of if they were to serve God properly.

24:24   The people agree and Joshua renews the covenant. So is this Eden restored? Will it last? Will Israel drive out the remaining pagans and live as God's holy people?

Judges

Chapter 1 gives an overview of how the conquest is going. There is plenty of success (e.g. v.4,9-11,17), but some difficulty too (e.g. v.19,21). Verses 27-35 are a list of failures of the Israelite tribes to take possession of the land. It seems that the Israelites grew weary of trying to rid the land of their pagan neighbours and failed to pursue the conquest promised to them. Instead they made treaties with their neighbours or made them labourers. They did not take seriously God's warning that they would be led astray from worshipping God if they lived amongst those who served pagan gods. This comes to a head in Judges 2.

2:1	God reminds them of what he has done for them.
2:2	God reminds them of their obligations and that their neglect of these is disobedience.
2:3	They are to bear the consequences of this disobedience. Now God will not drive them out and they will be a constant problem to the people of Israel for the rest of their history. They will become corrupted by the gods of the other peoples and worship them in addition to the God of Israel. In doing this they will offend God and reap his curses.
2:4	Although the people show repentance, there is no indication that God will change his mind. The period of the judges shows the blessings and curses in action.
2:8-15	Joshua dies.
2:10	'A generation emerges who do not know the LORD or what he has done for Israel.' (Note that the teaching of children during the festivals of Passover, Unleavened Bread and Consecration of the Firstborn were just some of the things God commanded to stop this ignorance taking root in Israel. It would seem that it was not just this generation who were disobedient.)
2:11-13	Failure actively to remember God and what he has done always leads to a steady drift towards doing what everyone else does. The Baals and Ashtoreth were the pagan gods and goddesses of Canaan.
2:14-15	Israel reaps the curses due for their disobedience.
2:16-18	God raises up a judge, a temporary leader through whom God delivers his people, and Israel is restored to the true worship of God for the period of his lifetime.
2:19	The judge dies and the people go back to their old unfaithful ways.

The time of the judges consists of this cycle being repeated over and over again, as illustrated by the accounts of Othniel (3:7-11), Ehud (3:12-30) and Deborah (4:1-24).

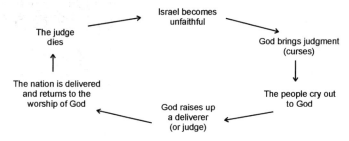

Why did they not believe in God's promises and fail to pursue the conquest? Why did they not teach their children as they were instructed? Why did they choose curses from God's hand rather than blessings? It is because they thought that their way was best. They thought that they were better able than God to make good plans for their future. They doubted God's promises and his goodness, just as Adam and Eve did in the Garden of Eden, and missed out on the opportunity to enjoy God's wonderful rest.

Lesson Summary

God promised to give the Israelites the whole land and told them to drive out the other nations. If they did this, they would be able to follow God and keep his law without distraction and so fulfil their calling as God's holy nation. However, they lost heart and did not trust God to give them victory. They allowed other nations with their pagan religions to live alongside them. God allowed them to take the consequences of their actions and these other religions constantly distracted them from worshipping God for the rest of their history. The time of the judges shows the blessings and curses of Deuteronomy in action. It also shows us that the only hope for God's people lies in God sending them a rescuer to deliver them and lead them back to the true worship of God.

Consequences

Everyone sits in a circle on a strong chair. The leader reads out statements one at a time, which require a response from various members of the group, such as, any boy wearing black socks move 4 places to the left, any girl with blue eyes move 3 places to the right, etc. When a statement is read out, the designated group members obey those instructions and move the required number of places. If someone is already sitting on the chair, the person sits on their lap. Whenever someone who has a player (or players) sitting on top of them is required to move, those players sitting on top move with them. Point out that obedience has consequences - and so does disobedience. In today's Bible study we will discover the consequences for God's people when they stopped obeying him.

Lesson Plan

1. Focus activity.

2. Make a list of statements which might describe the Promised Land, some true and some false. Cut up the list into strips with one statement on each. Divide into small groups and give a complete set of statements to each one. Get them to sort out which statements are true and which false.

Suggested statements:

True - a fertile land, full of fortified cities, full of pagan religions, full of other nations, produces beautiful grapes, produces beautiful figs and pomegranates, a good land, a land flowing with milk and honey.

False - produces coconuts, empty, full of Egyptians, full of rubbish, inhabited by giants, full of large factories.

After this task is completed, discuss whether or not it will be like Eden. Read Deuteronomy 8:7-9. This description of the Promised Land is interesting as it seems to suggest that it will be like Eden in some respects. However, the land is still full of locals worshipping pagan gods. Why is this a problem for Israel? What has God told them to do about it?

Recap on the blessings and curses, writing a selection down to refer to later in the lesson. Does the group think that they will take God's warnings seriously?

3. Read Joshua 13:1-7. How far has the conquest got? What has God promised? Read 21:43-45; 23:1. Draw attention to the significance of 'rest'.

4. Summarise Joshua's farewell speech in Joshua 23-24. You could do this by writing down:

ch.23	ch.24
Remind	God
Urge	Only God
Warn	Only God for Me

and saying a sentence about each point. This shows us clearly what the issues were in Joshua's mind as he prepared to leave them.

5. Read Joshua 24:19-24. Are Joshua's concerns about their ability to be faithful justified?

6. Give a short overview of Judges 1. Read Judges 2:1-4. What will this mean for Israel?

7. Read Judges 2:8-16,18-19 and draw the cycle of apostasy and rescue (see diagram on page 48). Point out the people's failure to remember anything about their God.

8. Read the story of either Othniel, Ehud or Deborah to illustrate the cycle. If time allows you could break into 3 groups and give each one one character to study and feedback to the group.

The time of the judges was a time of great instability. During this period there was growing pressure to have a king. When they lived in tents in the desert, the Tent of Meeting was in the centre of the camp in the place of the monarch's tent. Part of their distinctiveness was that God, rather than a man, was their king. But in Judges 8:22-23 the Israelites urge Gideon to be their king. He refuses saying, 'The LORD will rule over you.' He recognises that it would be inappropriate for him to rule the Israelites. God is their king.

Abimelech has no such scruples. In Judges 9 he tries to seize power and make himself king. Judges ends with the statement, 'In those days Israel had no king, everyone did as he saw fit.' This leads into the account of Samuel, the last of the judges, and on to the establishment of the monarchy.

1 Samuel

8:1-5	There seem to be 2 main reasons the Israelites want a king, one good - they do not want to be ruled by Samuel's corrupt sons - and one bad - they want to be like other nations (v.20).
8:6-8	God sees this request as a rejection of him. Just as they have rejected his authority over them from the very beginning, they now reject him as their king.
8:9-17	Samuel warns them as God has told him to. He points out all the disadvantages of having a human king rather than God.
8:18-20	It is amazing that they prefer to put their trust for success in battle in an essentially powerless king rather than in the LORD, who has shown himself throughout their history to be infinitely powerful and trustworthy. They had understandable reservations about Samuel's sons, but they had seen God work mightily through Samuel in recent victories over the Philistines. This was no mean feat, the Philistines being a formidable enemy and militarily more advanced than Israel. The warning in v.18 that God's help may be denied them in the future does not deter them.

God acknowledges that a king will bring trouble, but grants their request anyway. In fact, his instructions given to Moses in Deuteronomy 17:14-20 anticipate the call for a king and make provision for it. If Israel is to have a king, he should be the one God chooses. He must be an Israelite, not a foreigner, and must put himself under the authority of God. He must not acquire many horses (especially from Egypt) and must not take many wives. He must not accumulate large amounts of silver and gold and must not consider himself better than his brothers or above the law. These details are important, as they turn out later on to be the source of Solomon's downfall. Israel can have a king, but the appointment will be on God's terms. He will chose the King and appoint him.

Saul was the first King of Israel. He was chosen by God and anointed by Samuel. The Holy Spirit came upon him as a sign of God's presence with him. In OT times normal believers did not have the Holy Spirit living in them. The Holy Spirit only came upon certain individuals to equip them for a God-given role. It is only after the death of Jesus that all believers have the gift of the Holy Spirit (John 7:37-39). Things go well for Saul at first.

10:23-25	He was a big, impressive fellow and willing to be a king on God's terms.
10:27	Yet some despised him.
Ch.11	He has military success.
13:8-12	But he shows that he does not respect God's law concerning the sacrifices. He offers a burnt offering to ask the LORD's favour prior to a battle. He was not a priest and therefore not entitled to do this.
13:14	He shows that his heart is not God's and therefore, as stated in Deuteronomy 17, his kingdom will not endure.
15:1-3	God's instructions are quite clear.
15:4-7	The battle went well, but...
15:8-9	...Saul disobeyed God regarding Agag and did not destroy other things that he wanted to keep. He only obeyed the instructions he agreed with. This is not partial obedience, but disobedience.

15:10	God sees what Saul has done and what it means. Saul has turned away from God.
15:12	No longer is he a king under God's authority. He thinks of himself as the ruler of God's people and the rightful recipient of praise and honour for the victory.
15:13-15	Saul tries to make excuses for his sin by blaming other people (just like Adam and Eve).
15:24	Here we see the root of the problem - Saul fears the people more than he fears God.
15:26-29	The consequences of sin are devastating for Saul. God has rejected him as king and will give the kingship to a better man than him.
15:30	Despite this catastrophic news, Saul seems more concerned about keeping up appearances in front of the people. Note that he refers to God before Samuel as the LORD your God.

God has allowed Israel to have a king but one on his terms, whom he will choose. The king is to be someone who will live under God's authority and will lead the people in obedience and in the true worship of God. A proud king, who will not live under God's authority, will lead the people astray. Can any human king fulfil this role and avoid being corrupted like Saul? The answer is, 'Yes - David', whom we will study next session.

Lesson Summary

Despite having seen God work in mighty ways through the judges, the Israelites want a human king. They want a figurehead like other nations to lead them into battle. God says that this amounts to a rejection of him as their king. God knew this would happen and had made provision for it through the law. They can have a king, but God will choose him. The king of the Israelites must be one who lives under the authority of God and leads his people in obedience. Saul starts well but soon fails and is rejected by God. God will take away the kingdom from Saul and his descendants and give it to a better man.

Peer Pressure   Divide the group into threes or fours and give each small group a selection of magazines and some scissors. Ask them to cut out all the advertments containing brand names. Pin them up on a board. Discuss what makes the adverts successful and how they affect the group members. Lead into a short discussion on peer pressure. Is this a modern phenomenon or has it been an issue down through the ages? Let's see how peer pressure affected God's people in the time of Samuel.

Lesson Plan

1. Focus activity.

2. Draw the Eden diagram. Recap on how God wanted the whole world to know about him as they saw God's people living under God's authority, receiving his blessing. Ask if that was happening? Draw people in the land with a different colour pen (diagram 2). Describe how that distracted God's people from serving him alone and turned them away from following him. Cross out the God relationship. Get the group to remember what followed when the Israelites stopped worshipping God and how God's provision of a judge restored them for his lifetime.

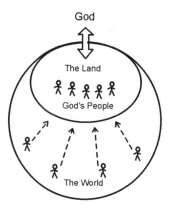

Diagram 1

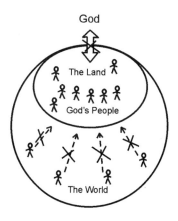

Diagram 2

3. Get the group to skim through the book of Judges and write down all the judges they can find. Point out how they were different from kings and why Israel did not have a king of their own. See what they remember about Samuel as the last of the judges.

4. Look at 1 Samuel 8, the call for a king. What was the reason they gave for their request? What was the real reason? How did God see things? What does Samuel do about it?

5. Look at Deuteronomy 17:14-20. Establish what kind of king would be suitable for God's people. Write these things down so you can see later how Saul went wrong.

6. Get the group to remember the first king - Saul - who he was, how he was chosen, what he looked like and his initial success. Make sure that they understand that he was God's chosen king. Samuel did not make a mistake.

7. Briefly describe the impending battle with the Philistines in 1 Samuel 13. Read 13:7b-10 and ask whether or not Samuel will be pleased with Saul and why? Read 13:14 and refer back to the warning in the Deuteronomy passage.

8. Read 1 Samuel 15:1-31. Compare Saul's behaviour and attitude to God with the list of qualities from Deuteronomy 17. What will God do about it? Who is the better man whom God will choose instead of Saul?

PREPARATION
1 Samuel 16 - 19, 2 Samuel 7

LESSON AIMS
To understand that David is God's chosen king through whom God's promise will be fulfilled.

Though God rejected Saul, he remained king for many years. In the meantime God sent Samuel to anoint another as king - a man after God's own heart (1 Samuel 13:14). God sent Samuel to anoint David, son of Jesse, who was only a youth at the time. In 1 Samuel 16 we read how God chose David from Jesse's sons, looking at his heart and not his outward appearance.

16:13-14   The Holy Spirit came upon David in power, but left Saul.

If Saul is characterised by his fear of man rather than God, David is characterised by his overriding concern for God's honour and his unshakeable faith in God. The story of David and Goliath illustrates this very well.

17:27   David is outraged that a Philistine should defy the armies of the Living God.

17:37   He is confident also that he will be delivered and God's honour restored.

Understandably, his fame spread and he became a saviour figure in the minds of the Israelites. This made Saul jealous. Saul had to live the rest of his life with 2 terrible burdens - firstly, knowing that he had been rejected by God and God's Spirit had departed from him and secondly, with the growing knowledge that David was God's chosen king. Even Saul's son and heir, Jonathan, recognised that David was God's Anointed, not Saul. Not surprisingly, all this proved too much for Saul to bear and we see the gradual disintegration of his personality throughout the rest of his life. Despite this David did not seek to become king whilst Saul was alive. On more than one occasion he was given the opportunity to challenge or kill Saul, but would not. He continued to be loyal to the king, even though Saul was trying to kill him. After the death of Saul and Jonathan in battle on Mount Gilboa, David was proclaimed King at age 30. He led a successful campaign against the Philistines, captured Jerusalem and made it his stronghold. One of the first things he did was bring the Ark of the Covenant into his city. This signified his commitment to God's rule and to the Ark as the symbol of God's rule. He wanted God to be seen to be living with his people and to experience the blessing that would bring. He wanted the worship of God to be at the centre of national life and the people to understand that he too lived under God's authority. The Ark was brought to Jerusalem with great rejoicing, David dancing before it.

God's Covenant with David (2 Samuel 7)

7:1   Here we have the 'rest' word again and must ask, 'Will this be Eden restored? God's people living in the land God has given, under God's authority?' God has given David great victories and the foreigners in the land have been driven out or subdued. Can David lead the people so that they will be faithful to God and experience the blessings promised? Will they be able to fulfil their part in God's plan to make him known to the nations?

7:2   David feels that the time has come to build a permanent sanctuary or temple for God.

7:5-7   Having a permanent sanctuary is not important to God.

7:8-11   God makes the same promises to David as to Abraham: hints at a special relationship (v.8), God will make his name great (v.9), a place for his people Israel (v.10).

7:11b   Instead of David making a house for God, God will make a 'house' for David. He will establish a dynasty.

7:12   David is promised a son (a son from his own body, again a clear allusion to the promise made to Abraham).

7:12-16   God gives David 4 promises which will be fulfilled through David's son.

1. God will establish his kingdom (v.12).

2. He will be the one to build a house for God (v.13).

3. He will have a special relationship with God, as father and son. There will be punishment for sin, but God's love will be permanent and unconditional (v.14-15).

4. His kingdom will last forever (v.13b,16).

These promises apply to 2 of David's sons. Partly they will be fulfilled through Solomon, who succeeded David as king. However, their ultimate fulfilment comes through Jesus, who was of the 'line' of

David and therefore a 'son' of David.

7:18-29	David's response to the promises.
7:18-21	David is aware of how great these promises are and he feels privileged to have had God make them known to him.
7:22-24	This is a neat summary of how God's 'name' was established. He took a people for himself and redeemed them from Egypt. He performed great and awesome wonders and established them as his very own forever. Look back at Exodus 6:6-8. This great definition of the LORD must have been in David's mind as he prayed this prayer.
7:26	Still David is concerned primarily for God's honour rather than for the honour of his family.

So a new pattern is established. God's king is the one through whom the covenant promises of God will be established. He is a kind of mediator figure like Moses, but also he is an authority figure whom God has set in place to rule over God's people forever.

Lesson Summary

David is God's king. He is chosen because his heart belongs to the LORD. He is concerned for God's honour in all that he does and is confident in God's promises. When he becomes king, David is not corrupted by his

position as Saul was, but brings the Ark to Jerusalem. He is king of Israel, but only under the authority of a greater King, the God of Israel. David is God's rescuer. In God's strength he defeats the enemies of God's people, in particular the Philistines, and so establishes rest on every side. God enlarges on his covenant promises made to Abraham. They will be fulfilled through David's son, who will rule God's people under God's authority forever. David sets a pattern for God's ultimate rescuing King - the Messiah or Christ. He will defeat finally all that opposes God and be made King forever. Through him God's rest will be permanently established.

FOCUS ACTIVITY

You Promised! Ask for volunteers to complete specified tasks for a reward. Suggested tasks are: 10 press-ups, hop the length of the room and back, piggy back a group member the length of the room and back, guide a blindfolded person through an obstacle course, keep a balloon in the air for 2 minutes only using your head, etc. Only reward some of those who complete their task successfully.

Discuss how they felt about only some people being rewarded. God is not like us - he always does what he says he will. In today's Bible study we will see what sort of king God chose to be the one through whom he would keep his promise to Abraham.

Lesson Plan

1. Focus activity.

2. Draw a crown. Ask the group why the people wanted a king and what the disadvantages would be. Record helpful answers on a board or flipchart. Draw another crown labelled, 'God's King'. See what they can remember about the instructions in Deuteronomy 17:14-20. How did Saul measure up? Why did God reject him? What has God said that he will do next?

3. Display some simple drawings of events in the early part of David's life and use them as prompts for the group to remember important things about David such as: The anointing of David; A harp; David and Goliath; Victory over the Philistines; Saul tries to kill David; Jonathan recognises David's anointing; Saul and Jonathan die in battle; David becomes king. (Pictures are available on page 88-89.)

   Do not spend too long on this. Fill in any of the important details they have forgotten, especially anything which underlines David's character, his concern for God's honour or evidence that God was with him.

4. The bringing of the Ark to Jerusalem. Show a picture of the Ark (see page 38) and get the group to remember what it was and what it signified. Recap on this story and ask why it was that David wanted the Ark in Jerusalem?

5. Read God's promises made to David in 2 Samuel 7:1-17. Elicit from the group the promises which are the same as the ones made to Abraham. Write them down and compare them. Do the same with the 4 promises which will be fulfilled through David's son. See if they know which son. Read Luke 1:68-75 to confirm that these promises are about Jesus.

6. Read David's prayer (or selected verses) to draw attention to his knowledge of God and his purposes, his concern for God's honour and his belief in God's promises. It may be useful to make the link between 1 Samuel 7:22-24 and Exodus 6:6-8.

7. Look at the list of the attributes of God's king made at the beginning of the lesson. How does David measure up? Will he be able to establish God's rest?

PREPARATION
1 Kings 2:2-5;
3:1-28; 4:20-34;
8:1 - 11:25

LESSON AIMS
To understand that Solomon, despite his wisdom, was not the one who would bring rest for God's people.

David was a good man and a good king, but was not perfect. He sinned by committing adultery with Bathsheba and then arranging for her husband Uriah to be killed. Also he failed to rule over his family adequately. His son Amnon raped his half sister Tamar and her brother Absalom killed him. Both Absalom and Adonijah, another son of David, tried to grab the throne for themselves. Despite these faults David is held up as a model of the ideal king and all subsequent kings are measured against him (e.g. 2 Kings 16:2; 18:3). David chose Solomon, son of Bathsheba, to succeed him. In 1 Kings 2:2-5 David charged him to keep the law of God and reminded him of the need for him and his descendants to walk faithfully before God to ensure that the throne of Israel stayed within their family.

1 Kings

3:1-3   Solomon starts well, loving God and obeying God's word. However, alarm bells are already ringing. He marries a foreign princess to bring about an alliance between Israel and Egypt. He sacrifices at a 'high place'. These high places were not exclusively associated with worship of the LORD, therefore Solomon sends a mixed message about worshipping the LORD alone. This contrasts sharply with the message David sent by bringing the Ark to Jerusalem.

3:4-9   Solomon asks for wisdom from God to be a good King.

3:10-13   God is pleased with him and promises to give him the wisdom he covets, as well as all the good things he might have asked for but did not.

3:14   The gift of long life depends upon him walking in God's ways (remember Deuteronomy 17:14-20).

3:16-28   Solomon exercises his God-given wisdom.

3:28   People recognised that the wisdom Solomon had was from God.

Chapters 4-10 tell us how God is fulfilling his covenant made with Abraham and David.

4:20   The people were very numerous.

4:21-24   The land was fully conquered.

4:24   There was peace on all sides.

4:29-34   Solomon had great wisdom in many areas. His knowledge of animals is noted, perhaps to remind us of Eden when Adam named the animals. He was so remarkable that people all over the world were drawn towards Israel.

This culminated in chapter 10, when the Queen of Sheba visits Solomon and is overwhelmed by what she sees and hears and praises God.

10:8   'How happy your men must be!... who continually stand before you and hear your wisdom!'

10:9   'Because of the LORD's eternal love for Israel, he has made you king, to maintain justice and righteousness.' This is a good example of how God's plan for Israel is intended to work. God's relationship with his people, through his king, brings blessing to them and other nations also - drawing them towards the God of Israel.

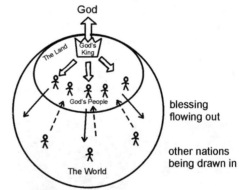

Chapters 5-7 record the building of the temple. But in chapter 9:4-9 Solomon gets a warning from God. God knows Solomon's heart. Perhaps all is not well.

11:1-3   Solomon goes down the same road as Adam and Eve. He thinks he knows better than God what is good for him and for Israel. He marries many foreign women, no doubt some for diplomatic purposes to bring stability to his country.

Nevertheless, this is breaking God's command. Furthermore, his loyalty seems to be towards his wives rather than towards the law of God.

11:4-6   They lead him astray, as predicted in Deuteronomy 17:17. But this is not all. Turn back to 10:23-29. Solomon accumulated great riches, in particular articles of silver and gold are mentioned here. Also Solomon accumulated horses, particularly mentioned are horses from Egypt. These things are specifically warned against in Deuteromomy 17:9-11. Although God had promised Solomon great riches (3:13), these blessings of God seem to have usurped God's place and become idols. God is angry with Solomon. Despite all that God had given him, he turned away from following God wholeheartedly. God will take the kingdom away from Solomon. Just like Adam, Solomon's disobedience would not just affect him but all who come after him.

11:12-13   However, out of love for his father David, God will not do it until after Solomon's death and David's family will be left with one tribe to rule.

Solomon had great wealth and great wisdom and made his country a major political player in the region. He completed a huge building project and did his best to ensure peace and stability for his subjects. However, the maintenance of his dynasty and the stability of his country would never be ensured by those things. He was required to keep God's covenant, but did not. So God did not give him a long life, (he was probably about 60 when he died), and afterwards dismantled all he had achieved. Once again sin had wrecked the ideal of God's people, in God's place, under God's authority. The rest of 1 Kings 11 tells of increasing unrest for Solomon. He has trouble from outside Israel in the form of Hadad, the Edomite, and Rezon, leader of a band of rebels in Aram, and rebellion from inside Israel from Jeroboam. The writer of 1 Kings is clear that these troubles come from God.

Lesson Summary

Solomon was enabled by God to extend the boundaries of Israel to their greatest limits and acquired great material wealth during his lifetime. God gave him great wisdom, which proved to be a blessing to the whole world and drew other nations towards Israel and her God. But he did not follow the Lord wholeheartedly as his father David had done. Just like Adam and Eve, he thought he knew better than God how to run his kingdom. He could not fulfil the promises made to David's son, because he would not live under God's authority. God judged him and his great kingdom crumbled after his death. It is nearly 1000 years before David's Son comes to bring in the Kingdom of God.

Discernment Divide the group into teams. For each team provide a pillow case tied at the top containing an identical selection of 10-20 different items. Give the teams 2 minutes to feel the items in their pillow cases, following which they must make a list of all the items felt. Once completed, the leader pulls the items out of a pillowcase one at a time for the teams to mark their lists. The team to identify the most items wins. Comment on the winning team's ability to use touch to discern which items were which. The Bible talks about the Christian's need to be able to discern right from wrong. Today's study is about a king, who asked God for the gift of discernment, so that he could govern God's people aright. Let's see how he got on.

Lesson Plan

1. Focus activity.

2. Ask the group to remember any nice things that have been said to them recently. See if any of them have been promised a treat or reward. Lead into the promises made to David and see if they can remember those made concerning David's son. To which Son of David did they refer?

3. Read 1 Kings 3:4-15 as a dramatic Bible reading, with group members taking the following parts: narrator, Solomon, God. What kind of king do we expect Solomon to be? Write down 'Solomon's Wisdom' on a board or flipchart. Read 3:16-28, again in parts - narrator, 2 prostitutes, Solomon. What is Israel's verdict on Solomon's wisdom?

4. Read 4:29-34 and 10:1-9, explaining that Solomon had built the temple in the intervening chapters. Discuss what effect Solomon's wisdom was having on other nations. How was that in line with God's plan? Use the diagram on page 54 to draw their thoughts together.

5. Write down 'Solomon Warned'. Read 8:56-61 and 9:1-9.

6. Write down 'Solomon's Folly'. Read Deuteronomy 17:14-20 and write down the main instructions, or produce the list made in previous lessons. Read 3:1-3; 10:26-29; 11:1-8. See how Solomon measures up. Discuss possible reasons why Solomon did not obey God's word and did not heed his warnings.

7. What will God do? Read 11:9-13 to see what God promises to do. Does that compromise his promise made to David?

8. Continue with the timeline to the division of the Kingdom. (Timeline Pages 81-87)

PREPARATION
1 Kings 11:26-40;12: 26-33; 15:1-16: 34, 2 Kings 17; 24 - 25

LESSON AIMS
To show that God judged his disobedient people in the way he had promised.

In this lesson we will cover the history of Israel from the division of the Kingdom in 922 BC to the exile of the Northern Kingdom in 722 BC and the Southern Kingdom in 587 BC. Solomon was told that, because his heart had turned away from the LORD and he had not kept the covenant, the kingdom would be torn out of the hand of his son and given to one of his subordinates. The subordinate in question was Jeroboam.

1 Kings

11:28	Jeroboam was an able man and a subordinate of Solomon.
11:31	God is going to use Jeroboam to bring about his judgment on Solomon.
11:34	Judgment will be deferred because of God's love for David.
11:36	One tribe, (plus the little bit of Benjamin that is left)., will be ruled by David's family.
11:37	This kingdom is given to Jeroboam by God.
11:38	If Jeroboam is obedient and walks in God's ways as David did, God will establish another godly kingdom through Jeroboam and his descendants.
11:39	Here is a glimmer of hope for David's kingdom and David's line.
11:40	Solomon was unable to interfere with God's plan for Jeroboam.

1 Kings 12 tells of the great foolishness of Rehoboam, Solomon's son, who succeeds him as king. Ten of Israel's tribes are already on the point of rebellion, due to the forced labour which had been exacted by Solomon, but they are ready to support Rehoboam if he will make things easier for them (12:4). His advisers tell Rehoboam that he should do as requested and those tribes would be loyal servants (12:7). But Rehoboam rejects their advice and instead takes the advice of his 'mates', who tell him to make the people work harder and treat them more harshly (12:8-11). This act of breathtaking arrogance causes the 10 northern tribes to rebel against Rehoboam and set up their own kingdom. They no longer want their future to be tied up with the house of David, but will go it

alone with Jeroboam as their king. But what kind of king will he be? Will he walk with God and receive the promises of 11:38?

12:26-27	Jeroboam is a king like Saul, not a king like David. He fears the people rather than God and wants their support for his reign, not God's. He does not lead the people in the authentic worship of God.
12:28-33	Instead Jeroboam sets up what amounts to an alternative religion in the north, with alternative places of pilgrimage at Bethel and Dan and alternative festivals. This is disastrous for the Northern Kingdom (also called Israel, the southern kingdom became known as Judah). They can never worship God acceptably on their own terms. This marks the end of any kind of purity of worship in the Northern Kingdom. Jeroboam had turned his back on the true worship of God and led his people into idolatry. All subsequent kings of Israel followed suit.

It is interesting to note small allusions to the Exodus story in this passage. Rehoboam responds to the northern tribes' request much as Pharaoh did to Moses. Jeroboam responds to his fear of the people as Aaron did, by making golden calves and announcing, 'Here are your gods, who brought you out of Egypt.'

15:25-26	Nadab, son of Jeroboam, did evil in the eyes of the LORD, walking in the way of his father and in his sin, which he had caused Israel to commit.
15:33-34	Baasha, having killed Nadab and all of Jeroboam's family, reigned for 24 years and did evil in the eyes of the LORD, walking in the way of Jeroboam and in his sin, which he had caused Israel to commit.

His son Elah was killed by Zimri, who proclaimed himself king and then killed Baasha's whole family. Omri was proclaimed king by the people and Zimri committed suicide. 1 Kings 16:19 says that he died because of the sins he committed, doing evil in the eyes of the LORD, walking in the way of Jeroboam and in his sin. Omri did no better (16:26).

The son of Omri was Ahab, who did more evil in the eyes of the LORD than any of those before him (16:30). We know more about Ahab than the other kings of Israel, because it was during his time that God raised up Elijah the prophet. Both Elijah and later Elisha were sent by God to the Northern Kingdom to warn the people, including the king, about the consequences of rejecting God.

That is not the prophets' only role. Since the kings have rejected God comprehensively they can no longer fulfil the role given to the king. They cannot be the channel for God's rule of his people. God raises up Elijah and Elisha to take on the role of national leaders and provide an alternative route to God. God does many miracles through them.

Miracles do not occur randomly throughout the Bible story. They occur mainly in 3 clusters and they are a sign that God's authority rests with the miracle-worker , so that the people will heed and believe God's word through him. The first cluster is around Moses, where God used miracles to show the Israelites that Moses was his man. The second cluster is around the ministries of Elijah and Elisha, where God showed the people that Elijah and Elisha were the ones speaking for him, not the king. The third cluster occurs in the NT and demonstrates God's authority through Jesus and the apostles.

Despite the ministry of Elijah and Elisha, Ahab continued to be a typical Northern Kingdom king, who would not follow God even though God's presence and power was demonstrated to him in unmistakable ways. His son carried on the family tradition (1 Kings 22:51-53). The Northern Kingdom had 17 kings and all of them were bad. Eventually Israel was invaded by the Assyrians and taken into captivity, from which they never properly returned (2 Kings 17:3-6). 2 Kings 17:7-23 gives a good summary of what happened to Israel and why.

Judah, the Southern Kingdom, consisted of the large tribe of Judah and the much smaller tribe of Benjamin. Despite having the temple and kings of the Davidic line, Judah did not fare very much better than Israel. The Southern Kingdom had 19 kings, five of whom were good and followed in the ways of David. Ten behaved in a similar way to the kings of the Northern Kingdom and four were good but weak. Under the good kings, like Hezekiah and Josiah, we find that there was hope for Judah. Generally the high places were removed and the idols destroyed. The good kings led the people back to the worship of God. However, none of them were of the same calibre as David and the change only lasted as long as the reign of the good king. When he died, just as in the time of the Judges, apostasy followed. 1 Kings 15:9-15 gives an account of King Asa, illustrating some of these things. In 597 BC the Babylonians, under Nebuchanezzar, invaded Judah.

2 Kings

24:10-11	Jerusalem is besieged.
24:13	The king is taken prisoner and the temple plundered.

When the next king, Zedekiah, rebelled against Nebuchadnezzar the Babylonians destroyed Jerusalem and its walls and burned the temple. They took with them all the silver, gold and bronze. Large items were broken up and carried away (2 Kings 25:8-17). They were taken to Babylon and put by Nebuchadnezzar in the treasure-house of his god (Daniel 1:2).

God's people had ignored all the warnings. They had not learnt from the example of Israel's exile. They had not responded to the prophets' warnings of judgment. (More of these in the next study.) They had thought that they were secure in their land. They had the temple and every day religious rituals were carried out. They kept the festivals as instructed and they thought that this would keep the LORD happy, even though many carried out other religious rituals to keep other gods happy also. They thought that God would not allow disaster to come upon them because that would bring dishonour on his name. They were wrong.

God had been absolutely serious about the blessings and curses in Deuteronomy. He had been absolutely serious about the warnings he gave to Solomon in 1 Kings 9:6-9. It was a catastrophe for God's people. Their national identity was based upon God's promises made to them through Abraham, Moses and David. Their foundations had been swept away. They no longer had a land in which to live as God's people. They no longer had a king from David's line, through whom God's promises were channelled, and no longer had a temple, where God was present and where they could worship him and atone for their sin.

Lesson Summary

Just as sin comprehensively wrecked 'rest' in the garden of Eden, so also it destroyed hopes of rest in the promised land. David was the only king of his kind and he was not perfect. Even the good kings of Judah did not measure up to the standard set by David and none of the northern kings followed the LORD. Instead of leading the Israelites in the true worship of God, their rules were harsh and promoted idolatry. This was not the life of rest in God's place, but a life more like slavery in Egypt. Both kings and people were unable to stay faithful to God and remained deaf to the warnings of God's messengers. This should not surprise us; the natural state of mankind is in slavery to sin. For people to want to follow God and not to turn away from his instructions, something needs to happen to them on the inside.

FOCUS ACTIVITY

Keeping the Rules

Play any well-known game with simple rules, such as tag or a simple relay race, and prime 2 or 3 people to continually break the rules. Allow the rule breakers to cause some disruption and ignore any adverse comments from the rule keepers.

Discuss how the group felt about some people getting away with breaking the rules. Did it cause other group members to break the rules as well? In the time of the Kings, God's people constantly broke his rules. Did they get away with it? Let's see what the Bible has to say about it.

Lesson Plan

1. Focus activity.
2. Draw 3 figures with crowns labelled Saul, David and Solomon. Get the group to remember their good and their bad points. What did God say he would do to/for each of them?
3. Get a piece of fabric and tear it in half. (It helps to make a small cut with scissors in advance.) Continue to tear it up into 12 pieces. Put 10 in one pile and 2 in another. Ask your group if they know what you are doing. Use this to lead into the Jeroboam story in 1 Kings 11:28-40.
4. Remind the group of Rehoboam's foolishness and how that caused the 10 northern tribes to rebel. Label the pile of 10 piece of fabric 'Northern Kingdom / Israel' and the 2 pieces 'Southern Kingdom / Judah'.

5. Ask what promises were made to Jeroboam if he ruled under God's authority (11:38)? Will he do it? Read 1 Kings 12:25-33 to find out what he did. Get the group to flick through the kings of Israel as far as Ahab, finding out what was said about them.
6. See what they remember about King Ahab and the prophets Elijah and Elisha. Describe Elijah's and Elisha's role in providing an alternative route to God.

   Despite God's messengers and the miracles they performed, Israel did not listen. Summarise how they were taken into exile.
7. Ask the group to find out who were the 5 good kings of Judah. Describe how similar their reigns were to the time of the judges. Read the account of King Asa in 1 Kings 15:9-15 to illustrate.
8. Give a quick summary of what happened to the Southern Kingdom. Describe the desolation they felt at the seeming loss of all that had been promised. Is this the end of God's plans for Israel?
9. Discuss why God's people were unable to be faithful and seemed so blind to all the warnings. Can they change by trying harder? What needs to happen to them?

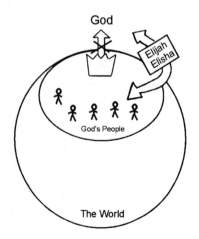

PREPARATION

See lesson notes

LESSON AIMS

To understand how the prophets fit into God's plan.

This lesson is a digression from the main Bible overview. Often young people are hazy about prophets generally and their purpose in God's plan. This leads to confusion when encountering 'prophecy' in a New Testament context. This lesson attempts to 'organise' prophecy as found in the Old Testament. It has to be an over-simplification, but will provide a useful framework.

Prophets in the Old Testament fall broadly into 3 groups:

1. The earlier 'non-writing' prophets, e.g. Samuel, Nathan, Ahijah, Elijah, Elisha.

2. The writing prophets from before the exile, e.g. Amos, Hosea, Isaiah.

3. The writing prophets from after the exile, e.g. Zechariah, Haggai, Malachi.

Some, like Ezekiel and Jeremiah, write mainly during the exile so fall between 2 and 3.

1. The non-writing prophets

We have already met some of these during the course. They were sent to speak God's word to the Israelites and their kings, to keep them serving God. They reminded them to keep the covenant given to them through Abraham and Moses. They rebuked them when they sinned and passed on God's warnings of judgment where appropriate (1 Samuel 15:26 - Samuel to Saul, 2 Samuel 12:7-12 - Nathan to David). Their job was to point people back to the Sinai Covenant, to remind them of their obligation to keep the law and to worship God only. If they did not, they would not be blessed and they would not be able to fulfil their function as the 'Kingdom of Priests', revealing God to the surrounding nations as God intended. Essentially they are prophets who look back.

2. The Pre-Exilic Writing Prophets

These prophets are raised up towards the end of the period of the monarchy, in the last 100 years or so before each kingdom was exiled. They are called writing prophets because their words were written down and now form part of the OT. They have a different message from their predecessors. Some were sent to the Northern Kingdom, e.g. Amos and Hosea. Some to the south, e.g. Isaiah and Micah,

and some did not start their ministry until the exile was almost upon them, e.g. Jeremiah and Ezekiel. But their message is much the same; it is a message of judgment. A devastating judgment is coming. Everything will be destroyed and their land will be taken away. Even God's presence will depart from them, leaving the temple empty. But it is also a message of restoration. This restoration will be centred around a new order, which will comprise the restoration of a king like David and the rebuilding of the temple, bigger and better than before. The hearts of the people will be changed so that they will no longer be hard. They will be able to serve God with all their hearts.

So there are 2 components to the message:
- devastating judgment
- permanent restoration.

Isaiah has them mixed together throughout his writing. Ezekiel and Jeremiah present the judgment first then the restoration at the end of their writings. Hosea acts out God's message by marrying an unfaithful woman to demonstrate the pain and betrayal God feels at Israel's unfaithfulness. Ezekiel often used bizarre and uncomfortable illustrations.

All these prophets look to the future, future restoration after judgment. They are not expecting God to put the covenant back the way it was before, but are looking forward to something new. This New Covenant will be initiated by God as the Old Covenant was, but it has bigger and better promises.

References which illustrate the coming judgment
- The unfaithfulness of God's people (Jeremiah 1:1-12).
- Exile for Israel in Assyria (Hosea 9:1-4 - Egypt is used as a reminder of the slavery they were rescued from).
- Judah's warning: They will go the way of the Northern Kingdom if they don't repent (Isaiah 10:10-11).
- Exile in Babylon predicted (Isaiah 39).
- God's people will be ejected from the land because of their unfaithfulness (Jeremiah 16:10-13).
- They should not trust in the temple to save them (Jeremiah 7:1-15).
- God will leave his temple (Ezekiel 10).
- The sanctuary will be desecrated (Ezekiel 24:20-24).

- Yet disaster may still be averted if they repent (Jeremiah 4:1-2).

References which illustrate the future restoration
- Restoration of the land and return from exile (Jeremiah 16:14-14; 29:10-14; 31:16-17).
- Restoration of a King like David (Isaiah 9:6-7; 11:1-5, Ezekiel 34:22-24, Jeremiah 23:5-6).
- Restoration of a bigger and more splendid temple (Ezekiel 40-47).
- The people of God will be changed on their return (Jeremiah 24:4-7).
- They will be cleansed so that they can truly serve him (Ezekiel 36:24-29).
- Jerusalem will not only be a centre of blessing to the world, but also people will stream to it (Isaiah 2:1-3).

The New Covenant (Jeremiah 31:31-34).
This New Covenant will be like the old:
a) God says, 'I will be their God and they will be my people' (v.33b).
b) at its centre will be the Law of God.

But not like the old (v.32):
a) God's law will be within them, written on their hearts and minds (v.33b).
b) God says, 'they will all know me' (v.34).
c) Their sins will be forgiven and their wickedness remembered no more (v.34b).
d) It will not be broken (implied in v.32).

Jeremiah does not give any explanation as to how it might be possible for a Holy God to forgive their sins and remember their wickedness no more, but this promise is foundational to the New Covenant.

Isaiah, in his 'servant songs', (Isaiah 42:1-4; 49:1-6; 50:4-9; 52 13 - 53:12), speaks of one who will bring justice and restoration. He will suffer as a 'guilt offering', bearing the sins of many. It is not clear how much Isaiah understood whom he was writing about. However, we can see that Isaiah's prophecy was looking forward to the death of Jesus in our place. Through him this wonderful promise of forgiveness would be fulfilled.

3. The post-Exilic Prophets
When the people returned from exile, (which will be covered in the next session), they found that things were not nearly as good as the promises they had been given. The function of these prophets was to draw attention to this fact. They were to tell the people that the promises had not yet been fulfilled, but they would be. They encouraged the people to stay faithful to their God and be patient while they waited for God to bring about what he had promised (Haggai 2:6).

Lesson Summary
A prophet is someone who speaks the words God has

given him. There are 2 main categories of prophet in the Old Testament. The earlier ones, who look back to the Sinai covenant and remind the people of their obligation to keep the law and to worship the LORD only, and the later ones, who look forward to restoration and the establishment of a New Covenant. Of these, the prophets from before the exile warn of terrible judgment to come followed by exile for God's disobedient people. This will be followed by a wonderful and permanent restoration. After the exile, when reality did not match what had been promised, the prophets encouraged the people to remain faithful and wait patiently for God to keep his promises in full.

True or False?   Place a large container on the table and a box containing a selection of common objects from a specified area, such as a kitchen. Choose someone to be the leader. While the remaining group members close their eyes, the leader places one of the items into the container on the table. The group members question the leader to discover which item is in the container. Before any questions are asked the leader must decide whether he/she will give all true answers or all false ones. After 5 questions have been answered the group must decide whether or not the leader is answering truthfully. Questions continue until someone correctly identifies the item. That person takes over as the leader. This game can be played by 2 teams. Points are awarded for correctly identifying whether the leader is giving true or false answers and for guessing the item in the container before the end of 20 questions. Comment on the need to identify whether or not the leader was telling the truth. What has this to do with today's Bible study?

1. Focus activity.

2. Ask, what is a prophet? Record the answers on a board or flipchart and ask the group to pick the right answer - a prophet is someone who speaks God's words. On strips of paper write the names of 25-30 Bible characters. Include Moses, Samuel, Nathan, Ahijah, Elijah, Elisha, Micah, Amos, Hosea, Zephaniah, Isaiah, Jeremiah, Ezekiel, Haggai, Zechariah and Malachi (all prophets). Make up the required number using other OT characters from Abraham onwards, e.g. Jesse, Isaac, Ishmael, Nebuchadnezzar, Jeroboam, Joseph, Solomon. Get the group to sort the names into prophets and non-prophets. Sort the prophets into the ones we have met so far on our Bible Overview and the ones we have not. (Nathan has not been mentioned, but he belongs in the first group.)

3. There is a lot of information in the teacher's notes. It is important to understand as much as possible, but to present the material at an appropriate level for your group. Be selective with the references you use. It is more important for them to understand the general drift of things rather than where to find each reference. In fact, the references given do not do justice to the words of the prophets, whose force comes through their many words and cannot be expressed adequately in a few 'proof texts'. Get the group to draw faces on the strips of paper of prophets' names, with the non-writing prophets facing left and the writing prophets facing right.

4. Get the group to put the non-writing prophets in order and go through where we met them in the OT story. Place another piece of paper with Mount Sinai drawn and written on it in front of Moses. Explain the function of the non-writing prophets and how they all look back to the Sinai Covenant. Remind the group of how God used Elijah and Elisha to become alternative national leaders when the kings were not doing their job and how he showed that his authority rested with them through many miracles.

5. See what the group know about any of the writing prophets. Divide the names into 3 groups: pre-exile, during exile and post-exile. Put the the post-exilic prophets to one side. We will talk about them in the next session. Explain the message of the pre- and exilic prophets, writing down the points so that the whole group can follow.

6. Divide the group into pairs and give each pair 1 or 2 references to look up and see which point they refer to. Feed back and tick off the list points for which references have been found. This is not a usual way to study the Bible, but it shows that the material presented is in the Bible and reinforces learning. It may be best to do this in 2 sections, judgment first and then restoration.

7. Study Jeremiah 31:31-34. Discuss how the new covenant is the same as and different from the old. How can God promise to 'forgive their sins and remember their wickedness no more'?

8. Read Isaiah 53. Who is this speaking of and how will sins be forgiven?

PREPARATION
Ezra 1 - 3; 6:13 - 7:10, Nehemiah 9 - 10; 13

LESSON AIMS
To understand that return from exile did not bring the promised restoration.

The Assyrians, who had overcome the Northern Kingdom in 722 BC, were conquered by the Babylonians in 609 BC. In 597 BC Judah was conquered by Babylon. The Babylonians took the royal family and leading citizens of Judah away into exile (including Daniel and his friends). They installed Zedekiah as the puppet King of Judah. However, Zedekiah rebelled against the Babylonians. They retaliated by destroying Jerusalem and the temple and by taking more people into exile.

So what was God doing? Were all his promises now defunct? We know that this is not true because the prophets were telling of the wonderful restoration that would come after the years in exile. Those who believed God's promises would have been heartened by this. But even in exile God was at work. He was continuing to bless and to look after his people and use them to make himself known to other nations.

The first half of the book of Daniel is about how Daniel and his friends were used to make the LORD known to the leaders of Babylon, Media and Persia. The king wanted to re-educate them and make them Babylonian, but they were determined to maintain their distinctiveness as God's people. Life became very difficult and dangerous for them at times as they refused to be integrated into the court of Nebuchadnezzar or to conform to the religious practices of Babylon, which would have compromised their faithfulness to God. They were very like David, concerned primarily for God's honour and confident in his power to deliver them. They endured the fiery furnace and the lions' den and, through these events, God showed himself to the Babylonians (and later to the Medes and Persians) to be a great and powerful God. It is possible that two foreign kings became believers in God, King Nebuchanezzar (Daniel 2:46-47; 3:29; 4:27) and King Darius (6:26-27). By their positions of influence Daniel and his friends were able to help keep the Jews safe.

Later Queen Esther was placed by God in a position where she was able to prevent a massacre of the Jews, after which they were protected and revered.

During their time in Babylon the prophets encouraged Judah to look on the exile as punishment from God for sin and to turn back to him. It seems they responded to this message. They had to live in Babylon, but maintained their distinctiveness and were faithful to God. When the Northern Kingdom was exiled in Assyria they were absorbed into the Assyrian Empire. They intermarried and were lost forever. Those from the Southern Kingdom remained a recognisable nation which could be restored. After 70 years Cyrus of Persia, who conquered Babylon in 539 BC, issued a decree allowing the Jews to return to Jerusalem.

Ezra

1:1	A prophecy in Isaiah 45:13 tells of Cyrus, whom God will raise up to rebuild his city and set his exiles free.
1:2	Other documents suggest that Cyrus did not believe in the LORD exclusively. Rather, he had great respect for the gods of his subjects and had a policy of repatriating their images rather than keeping them as trophies as his predecessors had done.
1:3	Encouraging the rebuilding of the temple in Jerusalem was probably part of this policy, although the reason he did it was to fulfil God's promise.
1:4-6	The provision of silver and gold for them to take with them is reminiscent of the Exodus. The freewill offerings are reminiscent of the building of the tabernacle.
1:7	From Cyrus' point of view, returning these items was similar to returning the idols of other nations. From the point of view of God's people, it was a sign that God's covenant could still continue. Once more they could have the sanctuary of God at the centre of national life.
3:2	One of the first to return to Judah was Zerubbabel, a descendant of David. He became leader of the Jews.
2:68-69	The first thing the returned exiles did was to collect a freewill offering from those in Jerusalem.

3:2	The next thing they did was to rebuild the altar of burnt offering as described in the law of Moses, so that they could begin sacrificing to the LORD once more and keep the religious festivals.
3:3	They did this despite intimidation from those around.
3:10-11	Then they started to rebuild the temple and there was much rejoicing when the foundations were laid. All seemed to be going well.
3:12-13	However, many of those, who remembered the old temple, wept because this new temple was so poor compared with the one which had preceded it.
6:13-18	There was opposition to the building by the enemies of Judah (chapter 4), as well as some laziness or reluctance on the part of the Jews at first, but eventually it was finished and dedicated to God.
6:19-22	The Passover and Feast of Unleavened Bread were celebrated. All was done 'according to what is written in the Book of Moses' (6:18).
7:1-10	Ezra the priest came to Jerusalem to be the High Priest. His ancestry could be traced back to Aaron and he devoted himself to studying and teaching the Law to Israel.
	Still all seemed to be going well.

The book of Nehemiah tells how God made it possible to rebuild the walls of Jerusalem, which was managed in a very short period of time, despite fierce opposition from Israel's enemies. When the walls were finished Ezra read the book of the Law to the people, who wept as they understood what was being read (Nehemiah 8:8-9). Then Ezra gave an overview of the history of Israel, just as Moses and Joshua did, prior to the people signing up once again to keep God's covenant.

Nehemiah

10:29	They promise to keep all the decrees of the LORD.
10:30	They promise to keep their distinctiveness by not intermarrying with other nations.
10:31	They promise to keep the sabbath.
10:32-39	They promise to support the temple, its priests and its activities.

All seems to be going very well indeed. Will they this time, having been punished in exile, keep faithful to their God and receive his blessings? Later, Nehemiah made a visit to Babylon to report to the king and when he returned things were not so great.

13:10-11	The temple had been neglected.

13:15-16	The sabbath was not being kept.
13:23-24	There had been intermarriage with surrounding nations.

The people had not changed. They were as rebellious as ever, reverting to doing things their own way, not God's way. The prophets had said that, when the people returned from exile, things would be wonderful and the land would be restored to them, whereas in reality it's full of powerful and aggressive neighbours. They would be ruled over by a king like David, but in reality they are a small province in the Persian empire. Zerubbabel may be their governor, but he is not king. The temple would be bigger and better than what came before, but in reality it is much poorer than the one built by Solomon. The people would return from exile with changed hearts to know the Lord, but in reality they are just as rebellious as they have always been.

So what of the promises? Did God get them wrong? No, they refer to something further in the future.

What do the post-exilic prophets have to say? They say to be patient and God will fulfil his promises. Haggai actually draws attention to the fact that the new temple is not as good as the old one (Haggai 2:3), but tells them that this is only a beginning. God will keep his promises, all nations will come and God will fill the temple with his glory (Haggai 2:4-9).

The promises of restoration did not refer to the geographical land of Israel and its physical inhabitants. They are looking forward to the New Covenant that Jesus brings. Jesus is the King of David's line whose kingdom will endure for ever. Jesus' body is the new temple, more glorious and perfect than those which came before (John 2:18-22). Jesus is the one through whom it will be possible for God to forgive sins and remember wickedness no more.

Lesson Summary

When the people of Judah were taken into exile, it seemed to them that all their hopes lay in ruins, but God was still at work. Their time in exile chastened them and they did not lose their distinctiveness, as those from the Northern Kingdom had done in Assyria. God still cared for them and protected them and used them to reveal himself to their captors. When they were allowed to return to their land they expected the restoration of their fortunes just as the prophets had foretold. The reality was much less rosy. The prophets told them that the restoration of God's Kingdom was still in the future and they needed to be faithful and wait.

A Disappointing Result Divide the group into 2

teams and play a game such as balloon netball. Goals are scored by the goalie catching the balloon in a wastepaper basket or bucket. After a set period of time, stop the game and transfer the strongest players from the winning side onto the other one. This will ensure that the losing side is the eventual winner. Discuss how the side that was winning felt when they lost their strongest players. Comment on the disappointment we feel when a hoped-for event does not come to pass. In today's Bible study we will see what happened when God's people returned from exile and whether or not this brought about the fulfillment of God's promises.

Lesson Plan

1. Focus activity.

2. Recap on the promises made to Abraham. How were they enlarged upon through Moses and through David? Remind the group that God's people have been exiled and their land overrun. What has happened to the promises now? Try to elicit as many of the following as possible from your group. The promises can be crossed out as you go.

- ◆ Their land has gone.
- ◆ The nation is scattered.
- ◆ Their name is not great.
- ◆ They are not an obvious source of blessing to anyone.
- ◆ The temple, the sign of God's presence with them, has been desecrated and dismantled.
- ◆ They are not able to be a kingdom of priests or a holy nation.
- ◆ They are unable to perform the sacrifices to atone for sin.
- ◆ The promises about David's house reigning forever have come to nothing.

Only 400 years previously, David had been on the throne and Israel was a major world power. Now their hopes lie in ruins. Psalm 137 gives us an idea of the weeping and bitter emotions experienced by those who were deported. Lamentations 1:1-6 gives a desolate picture of what it felt like to be left behind.

3. Outline what happened to the Northern Kingdom after they were exiled. Contrast this with what happened to the Southern Kingdom in exile. Produce flash cards with the names of Daniel and his friends and Esther on them.What can the group remember about them? Outline how God used them in his plan.

4. Read Isaiah 43:13. What is Cyrus going to do? Read Ezra 1 to see how this was fulfilled. How would you have felt about this if you had been a Jew?

5. Describe what happened when the exiles returned. Produce more flash cards with Zerubbabel, Ezra and Nehemiah on them. This will give you some structure and help you elicit some of the story from the group.

6. Read Nehemiah 10:28-39. Write down the things that the people promise to do. Read Nehemiah 13:4-24, (or exerpts from), to see what happened when Nehemiah went away.

7. Look back at the promises of restoration after the exile. Have they been fulfilled? Has God gone back on his word? What do the prophets say? Read Haggai 2:1-9. What is God doing?

Week 21
Review of the Old Testament

PREPARATION

Old Testament

LESSON AIMS

To understand God's plan portrayed in the Old Testament and how this looks forward to New Testament events.

Lesson Plan

Reviews are important, but can be deadly boring. The best kind are stimulating and fun.

1. Names on backs game. On the back of each group member place a sticky label with the name of a major Old Testament character. Choose ones that have been studied during the course, so that your group will know something about them. The aim is to find out who they are by asking other group members questions, which can only be answered Yes or No. When they all know who they are, they line up in chronological order.

2. Divide the group into teams and give each team a set of small pieces of paper with Old Testament characters and events on them. Each team has to put them into chronological order. Also give them 4 pieces of coloured paper with 'Promise' written on them, which should be inserted where God made covenant promises (Abraham, Moses, David, Exile) Finally, give them another set with quotations from the characters. They have to line up the quotation with the character, e.g.

Adam:	'I heard you in the garden, but I was afraid because I was naked; so I hid.'
Men of Babel:	'Let us make a name for ourselves.'
Abraham:	'Will a son be born to a man 100 years old?'

Pharaoh:	'I do not know the LORD and I will not let Israel go.'
Joshua:	'As for me and my household, we will serve the LORD.
Saul:	'I was afraid of the people and so I gave in to them.'
David:	'Who is this uncircumcised Philistine that he should defy the armies of the living God?'
Solomon:	'Give your servant a discerning heart to govern your people.'
Daniel:	'My God sent his angel, and he shut the mouths of the lions.'

The first team to complete the exercise correctly wins.

3. As a group, go through what they have done in no.2, getting them to make corrections where necessary and telling the story as you go through. Make a graph of the fortunes of Israel over time. The graph should end up looking something like the one shown below.

Add in another line to show the scale of the promises (see page 66). Remind them that, at the end of the Old Testament, the promises have got bigger, but the reality does not match up. We are waiting for the New Covenant to deliver what God has promised.

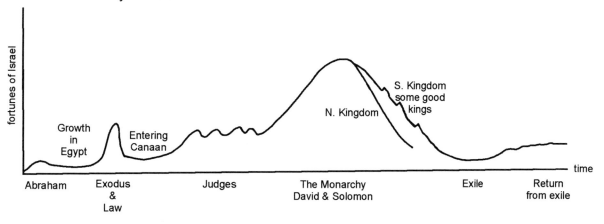

4. Compile a quiz on the Old Testament, which can take place in teams. Each team needs an A4 sheet of paper. When a team answers correctly they can draw or write the name of something that went in the tabernacle or its courtyard on their paper, e.g. Ark of the Covenant, lampstand, High Priest, etc., without showing you or other teams what they have put. At the end of the quiz total up the marks. Award 2 points for articles that go inside the tabernacle, 1 point for things which could be found in the courtyard and 1/2 point for dubious items.

5. Bible Timeline (Timeline Pages 81-87). You need one can of soft drink or similar for each event on the Old Testament section of the timeline. Use a permanent marker pen to write one date on the bottom of each can. Prepare a paper sleeve for each can containing the name of the person or event. Place the cans in the middle of the table and ask the group to put them in the correct order to make the timeline. Look at the dates on the bottom of the cans to check if it is correct. This can be done as a team activity.

6. Review the first 4 memory verses.

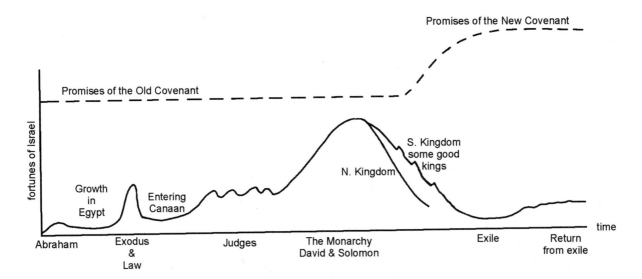

PREPARATION
Matthew 1:1 - 4:25

LESSON AIMS
To see that Jesus is the one promised in the Old Testament.

The last book of the Old Testament is the book of Malachi, following which there are 400 years of silence. Kingdoms came and went and the land of Israel remained a small and unimportant backwater within a larger empire. They were never self-governing and independent again until 1947. Many Jews did not return from exile but settled in other lands, taking their faith in God and their synagogues with them. Gentiles in those places started to hear of Israel's God and started to worship him. The Jews were waiting for God's rescuer to come, one who would liberate them from foreign domination and make their nation great again. They thought that he would be a great king, like David, and bring in another golden age for Israel.

The gospel accounts of Jesus' life will be very familiar to your group, but they will be able to see some things afresh, having understood more about the Old Testament background. We will study Jesus' life from the book of Matthew. Matthew wrote mainly for Jews and points his readers to the significance of the New Testament events in the light of the Old. In fact, it was probably placed first in the New Testament because of its continuity with what comes beforehand.

The first question Matthew addresses is, who is Jesus and where does he come from?

1. Jesus comes from Abraham and David.

The genealogy in 1:1-17 shows that Jesus comes from Abraham and David. When we studied Genesis we saw how the writer used genealogies to show links between important characters and which line they came from. At the beginning of his gospel Matthew wants to show us where Jesus comes from. He links Jesus to both Abraham and David.

1:1   Jesus is the Son of David. He is the son who fulfils the promises made to David. Jesus is the Messiah, the King of David's line who they have been waiting for. Jesus is the son of Abraham, the one who fulfils the promises made to Abraham.

1:2-6   The genealogy from Abraham to David.

1:6-11   The genealogy from David to the exile. The kingly line of David peters out here with the end of the monarchy.

1:12-16   After the exile David's descendants lead to Jesus.

1:16   The end of the genealogy is unusual, preparing us for the virgin birth.

1:17   Strictly speaking there are not 14 generations. Certain individuals have been left out (look at v.11). Matthew presents it like this to make a point. The Old Testament hangs around these events, the promises made to Abraham, their partial fulfilment and further promises made to David, the disaster of the exile, leading to their final fulfilment in Christ.

2. Jesus came from God and is the one promised by the prophets.

Matthew does not record the actual birth of Jesus. Again, he is more interested in where Jesus came from.

1:18   He was conceived by the Holy Spirit.

1:20   Joseph is referred to as 'son of David'.

1:21   The name Jesus is the same name as Joshua and means 'Yahweh is salvation'. Matthew wants us to know right at the beginning what kind of saving Jesus has come to do.

1:23   Throughout these passages Matthew is anxious to point his readers to OT passages authenticating Jesus as Messiah. Here he refers to Micah 5:2.

1:24   Joseph's actions show that he believed that Mary had done nothing wrong and that the child was indeed from the Holy Spirit. In naming the child Joseph is owning him, saying, 'He's mine.' This is how Jesus comes into David's line, despite Joseph not being his biological father. (Mary was also a descendant of David, but 'lines' passed through the male side of a family.)

3. Jesus is the new King like David.

In Matthew 2:1-12 we read of the coming of the Magi. These eastern people were almost certainly Gentiles, who knew something of the Jewish scriptures and faith. They were given the right instructions from the priests and teachers of the Law - Messiah would be born in David's home town and would follow the pattern of David's line, becoming a great King but also a shepherd and saviour of the people.

4. Jesus is a rescuer like Moses.

The story of the Magi is followed by the escape to Egypt. Just as Pharaoh gave the order for all Israelite male babies to be killed, Herod gives the order for all male babies in Bethlehem to be killed. But God rescues Jesus, just as he rescued Moses.

2:20   This is almost identical to God's instructions to Moses in Exodus 4:19. Again, Matthew is identifying Jesus with Moses.

5. Jesus is the LORD, coming to establish his Kingdom.

6. Jesus is the 'Servant' from Isaiah's prophecies.

Both of these points are brought out in the story of John the Baptist in chapter 3.

3:2   In saying that the Kingdom of Heaven is near, John the Baptist is announcing that the rule of God, as foretold by the prophets, is imminent. This is a big announcement!

3:3   This scripture from Isaiah is speaking of the LORD coming. John is preparing for the arrival of Yahweh himself. Jesus is God.

3:11   The coming one will baptise, not with water, but with the Holy Spirit. This is another big promise. Under the old covenant, the Holy Spirit only came upon certain individuals to enable them to fulfil certain roles. This is a fulfilment of the promise God gave through the prophet Joel, that God would pour out his spirit on all people.

3:17   These words from heaven identify Jesus as the 'servant' from the servant songs in Isaiah (42:1), but the voice identifies the servant as his son.

Secondly, Matthew looks at what Jesus has come to do, which will be dealt with in detail in the next session.

Jesus has come to identify with his people.

1. By being baptised by John as if he were an ordinary sinful Israelite.

2. By being tempted in the wilderness like the Israelites were.

4:1-2   This is all very reminiscent of the Israelites' time in the wilderness after the Exodus, when the Israelites were tested and continually found wanting. They complained about the food, they wanted to go back to Egypt and failed to enter the land when God brought them to its borders. In some senses Jesus is reliving the experiences of Israel. He was tempted in

similar ways, yet did not fail. The scriptural responses to the temptations are all quotes from the book of Deuteronomy, showing us that Jesus had these events in mind as he answered the tempter.

Lesson Summary

At the beginning of his gospel Matthew wants us to know who Jesus is.

He is - the one the Jews have been waiting for,

     - the Messiah, the Son of David, who will restore the fortunes of God's people,

     - a rescuer like Moses,

     - the servant described in Isaiah's prophecies,

     - from God, but he is also God,

     - the LORD, who is coming to establish his Kingdom forever.

Who is it? Give each group member 2 pieces of paper and a pen. On one piece of paper they write the numbers 1 to 6 down the left-hand side. Read out the following 6 statements for the players to record their answers.

1.   What is your favourite colour?

2.   What is your favourite school subject?

3.   What is your favourite pop group?

4.   What is your favourite food?

5.   What is your favourite TV programme?

6.   What is your favourite animal?

The players write their names on the bottom of the papers and fold them over before placing them in a container at the front. The leader takes the papers out of the container one by one, reads out the 6 answers and asks the group to identify the person concerned. This can be done verbally or by writing the answers down on the second piece of paper. If the answers are written down you need to go over the answers at the end to see who got most right.

Discuss how easily they were able to identify the other group members from a set of statements. Let's look at what statements the Bible makes about Jesus and see how well these correspond to what was predicted in the Old Testament.

Lesson Plan

1. Focus activity.

2. Write down the name of your group at the top and 'Who is Jesus' in the middle of a sheet of paper and 'brainstorm'. Write down all the answers given by the group. On another sheet write 'Who is Jesus' and write Matthew at the top in place of the group's name. Add to this sheet as Matthew tells us who Jesus is.

3. Look at the genealogy. What is Matthew telling us about who Jesus is in v1? Look through the names and see how many they recognise and can identify. How does Matthew organise his genealogy? Which Old Testament events is he drawing our attention to? These events are all associated with covenant promises - the covenant with Abraham, the one with David and the New Covenant promised at the time of the exile.

   Which important covenant is missing? (The Covenant with Moses.)

   What is Matthew telling us about Jesus through this genealogy?

4. Divide your group into twos or threes and get them to look at the birth of Jesus, the visit of the Magi and the escape to and return from Egypt.

   Are there any Old Testament events Matthew is wanting his readers to recall? This is hard. To make it easier show them a sheet of paper with some Old Testament events written randomly on it. Include all the ones you want them to think of, as well as some decoys.

   Once they have made the OT links the follow up question will be much easier. What does Matthew want to tell his readers about who Jesus is?

   Get the group to suggest additions for the 'Who is Jesus' chart.

5. Read Matthew 3:1 - 4:11 and ask the same 2 questions. Give them time to think, but be prepared to lead them to the answers. Thinking in a fresh way about familiar portions of the Bible is hard. Reinforce the teaching by getting them to contribute to the 'Who is Jesus' chart.

Week 23

Why Did Jesus Come?

PREPARATION

Matthew 4 - 5; 8 - 9; 16:13 -17:13; 20:17-28

LESSON AIMS

To understand what Jesus came to do.

This lesson covers a vast amount of Jesus' teaching, so we have to organise the material to make it understandable, manageable and memorable. Jesus has come to establish the Kingdom of Heaven - the ultimate rule of God - to bring in the perfect pattern of God's people, living under God's authority in the place of God's provision. We focus on 4 aspects of this. They do not form a comprehensive account, but are presented in roughly the order they come in Matthew's gospel.

Jesus has come:

1. to call disciples (4:17-22), the true people of God (12:46-50),

2. to fulfil the Law (5:17-18 and the following sermon on the Mount),

3. to bring Rest (11:28-29),

4. to die as the ultimate guilt offering (16:21; 17:22-23; 20:17-19).

1. Jesus has come to call disciples (4:17-22)

4:17	At first glance Jesus' message looks very like John's and not dissimilar from that of previous prophets.
4:19	The difference is that Jesus calls people, not to turn back to God and walk in his ways, but to follow him, to be his personal disciples. They will become 'fishers of men' and are sent out to make the whole world Christ's disciples (28:19-20).

Chapter 5 continues this theme.

5:3-11	These true followers of Jesus will not have an easy time now, but they should be glad because:
	a) they are following in the path of the true servants of God, the prophets.
	b) there will be a future reward in heaven.
5:13-16	these verses imply that they will be a blessing to the world as they exercise their discipleship.

Who is the true family of God?

10:1-4	The answer is not the physical descendants of Jacob/Israel. Jesus chooses 12 men to whom he gives special authority. He commissions a new

nation of Israel, with these men replacing the 12 sons of Jacob.

12:46-50	The answer is not blood relations, but those who follow Jesus.

2. Jesus has come to fulfil the Law (5:17-24)

5:17	Jesus says he has not come to do away with the law. The covenant is built on the law.
5:20	This would have been puzzling. The Pharisees tried hard to keep every part of the law. It would be difficult for a Jew to imagine how an ordinary person could keep the law more perfectly than them. In the sermon on the Mount which follows, Jesus explains that God is not interested merely in keeping rules, but is concerned with the state of a person's heart. The heart is at the root of the problem.
5:21-24	Here is the first illustration of this. It is not just the act of the murder which is offensive to God, but the angry heart which underlies it. It is no use coming to God with a gift, but with a heart which is not right. This is what the Pharisees do and that is not good enough for God.

How will Jesus fulfil the law? He will enable them to keep it in a different way from the Pharisees - in a 'New Covenant' way. Remember Jeremiah 31:33. The law will not be an external thing, but will be written on their hearts. Obeying the law will not be avoiding certain actions, but of having a heart responsive to God. Good actions will flow from this. How Jesus will achieve this changed heart is not yet made explicit.

3. Jesus has come to bring Rest (11:28-29)

Rest implies restoration of the Eden experience. In 8:23 - 9:34 Jesus performs a series of miracles, which give us small glimpses of his power to restore the chaotic, fallen world, reversing the effects of the fall, e.g:

♦ the calming of the storm - power to restore the fallen natural world,

70

- the healing of the demoniac - power over rebellious spirits,
- the sick woman - power to heal,
- the dead child - power to reverse death,
- the paralytic - power to forgive sins.

These miracles set the scene for 11:28-29. On one level Jesus is talking about freedom from the huge religious burdens placed upon them by the Pharisees and others. At another level he is promising that final rest when he will undo the consequences of the Fall and bring permanent restoration.

4. Jesus has come to die (16:21; 17:22-23; 20:17-19)

20:28   Jesus is a servant and comes to give his life as a ransom for many. This verse takes us right back to the Servant of Isaiah 53. Jesus is the one who pours out his life unto death(Isaiah 53:12), his life is made a guilt offering (Isaiah 53:10) and he will bear the sins of many(Isaiah 53:12).

16:13-23   But Jesus does not tell his disciples what he has come to do until they have grasped that he is the Christ, or Messiah. There is a lot of speculation amongst the Israelites as to who Jesus might be. They centre on him being a prophet. No-one thinks of him as a King. This makes Peter's confession remarkable.

The Jews thought of the Messiah as a king, who would wield political power and win great battles. Clearly Jesus is not like this. God is at work in Peter, otherwise he could not have made this connection (16:17).

16:21   Jesus tells them what kind of Messiah he is going to be - one who suffers, is rejected and is killed. He will rise from the dead on the third day, but Peter has not got past the rejection and death part. He understands that the Messiah is going to be different from what they had expected, but not that different!

The account of the transfiguration comes next. It is essentially reassurance that Jesus is who he said he was. The situation of the mountain is reminiscent of Sinai, where both Moses and Elijah had encounters with God. The change that comes over Jesus is similar to the glory which was seen in the face of Moses. The cloud takes us back to Exodus also. The voice from the cloud tells the disciples to listen to him, meaning Jesus, rather than primarily to the law or the prophets, represented by Moses and Elijah.

Matthew records 2 further occasions when Jesus speaks of his death to his disciples (17:12-13; 20:18-19). Each time he speaks he adds more detail to the suffering picture. There is no indication that the disciples understand about the significance of the promised resurrection after 3 days.

Lesson Summary

Jesus has come to call disciples. He does not encourage them to turn back to God, as John did, but to follow him personally. They will form the basis of a new community of God's people. He will fulfil the law and will enable it to be written on his people's hearts. He will die as a permanent offering for sin, bringing true forgiveness and reversing the effects of the Fall, so that God's rest may be permanently re-established.

Rescue Designate an area to be the prison with a wall, chair, or similar that the prisoners must touch while they are in prison. Play a game of tag with several leaders being 'It'. Whenever a player is tagged he/she must go to the prison and stand touching the wall. If an uncaught player tags the prisoner he/she is released and rejoins the game. This game can be played in teams. Divide the group into 3 or 4 teams and play each round with a different team as the catchers. Each round lasts for the same amount of time and the number of prisoners at the end of the round is recorded. The team that catches the most prisoners wins. Comment on the prisoners inability to rescue themselves. In the same way we are unable to rescue ourselves from the penalty of sin. Let's see what the Bible has to say about our rescuer.

1. Focus activity.

2. Re-run the 'Who is Jesus?' activity from last lesson, to see what they remember about who Matthew says Jesus is. You can use letter prompts on the sheet to aid memory, e.g. 'a R(escuer)', 'like M(oses)'.

3. Prepare a board or sheet of card with the words, 'What has Jesus come to do?' in the middle of it. Write the 4 answers on each corner, but cover them with opaque card or paper stuck on with blutack. Begin this part of the lesson by inviting suggestions as to what Jesus has come to do. When someone guesses correctly they can uncover their answer on the board. When all 4 are revealed you have a visible structure for your lesson.

4. The amount of detail you include in each section will depend on the age and Bible knowledge of your group. They do not need to understand, or be presented with, all the material in the notes, but they do need to understand that Jesus did not just come to teach and heal, but to do a very specific job.

5. Read Jeremiah 31:31-34 to show that Jesus has come to establish the New Covenant, as promised by Jeremiah and the other prophets of his time.

When Jesus first reveals to his disciples he is the Messiah, the Christ, he says not to tell anyone. In the events leading to his death he wants all to know who he is.

Matthew 21

Jesus rides into Jerusalem on a donkey to fulfil the Messianic promise of Zechariah 9:9. He challenges the authority of those who run the temple and criticises their practices. The children shout, 'Hosanna to the Son of David', implying that Jesus is the King, the long awaited Messiah. Jesus conveys to the indignant religious leaders that they are right to sing of him in this way.

Matthew 23

Jesus is openly critical of the religious leaders and their religion of behaviour aimed to impress men rather than serve God. He condemns them for the burden they place on others, how they try to stop others entering the Kingdom. He uses strong words indeed. It is not surprising that the religious leaders plot to kill him (26:3-5). However, they are not in charge of events - God is - he decides the time of Jesus' death, not them (26:1-2,6-12).

The Last Supper (26:17-30)

This was a Passover meal. As we see in 26:1-2, Jesus already knew that this was the occasion for his death. We studied the Passover and its remembrance meal in Exodus 12 (Week 9). The preparations for the Passover meal involved getting a lamb that had been ritually slaughtered at the temple and its blood poured out on the sides of the altar. The lamb was taken home, roasted and eaten with unleavened bread and bitter herbs. During the meal 4 cups of wine were passed round and drunk. Between the drinking of the 1st and 2nd cups of wine the story of the Passover was recounted as a dialogue between father and son (or suitable substitutes). Originally the meal was eaten standing up, dressed for a journey, as instructed in Exodus 12. By the 1st century this custom had been abandoned and Jesus and his friends reclined to eat in the Roman way. (There is an outline of a simplified Passover meal in Book 2, Week 1.) Jesus uses this Passover meal to teach about his death.

26:26   Normally the unleavened bread would have been used to remind participants of the escape from Egypt. Jesus is reinterpreting it, using it to point to the future and his broken body.

26:27-28   Jesus uses one of the cups of wine to speak of his blood. He has 3 images in mind as he speaks these words.

♦ The Passover lamb - just as the blood of the Passover lamb was poured out over the altar, so Jesus' blood will be poured out. Like the Passover lamb he will die so that others may be spared.

♦ The Suffering Servant of Isaiah 53, who poured out his life for many as an offering for sin (Isaiah 53:10,12).

♦ The New Covenant described in Jeremiah 33:31-34, inaugurated with his blood.

Jesus takes this familiar meal, which pointed back to the Covenant with Moses, and uses it to point forward to his death as a 'sacrificial lamb'.

Trial before the Sanhedrin (26:57-67)

There was only one piece of evidence presented to the Sanhedrin. Allegedly Jesus had said, 'I am able to destroy the temple and rebuild it in 3 days.' We do not know if Jesus said these exact words. In John's account (John 2:19) Jesus said, 'Destroy this temple and I will rebuild in 3 days.' We know that Jesus was talking about his death and how it would make the temple obsolete. When his perfect sacrifice was made there would be no need for sacrifices, a sanctuary or curtain, because the way to God's presence would be open. However, the temple was all important to the religious leaders, as it was their power base. Already Jesus had seemed to threaten the temple when he cleared it. They were not taking chances; they were determined to get rid of him, so were not interested in anything else he had to say.

The Death of Jesus (27:32-54)

27:35   This points to Psalm 22:18.

27:39   Points to Psalm 22:7.

27:40   This is loaded with irony. He is destroying the temple indeed as he hangs on the cross. He could come down but does not, in order to be obedient to his Father.

27:41-42   More irony. They are exactly right. The

nature of his sacrificial work means he cannot save others and save himself too.

27:43   Points to Psalm 22:8.

27:46   Jesus' cry from the cross tells us of the agony he was experiencing as he took the punishment for sin. It is also the first line of Psalm 22.

27:51   The temple curtain, which barred the way into the Holy of Holies, was destroyed in a way no human hand could have accomplished. This signified that, at the point of Jesus' death, the way into God's presence was opened up.

27:54   In some ways this is the climax of the passage. A Gentile soldier and those with him respond to the death of Christ with awe and belief. Jesus has become the one through whom there is access to God. God's people are those from any nation who receive forgiveness through Jesus and become his disciples.

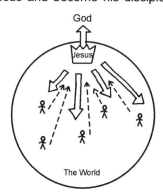

The Resurrection and Great Commission (28:1-20)

The resurrection of Jesus shows that all he has said about himself is true and all his words can be relied upon. In his account Matthew focuses on:

- the empty tomb and its consequences (v.11-15 - the great cover-up),

- the resurrection of the Lord and its consequences (exhilarated and bewildered believers being given their great commission).

God has given all his authority to Jesus. There is now no way to be God's people except though Jesus. There is no alternative route to God, which by-passes Jesus, so all nations must become his disciples. The New Covenant name of God is now 'The Father, the Son and the Holy Spirit.'

Lesson Summary

Jesus is the Messiah. As he enters Jerusalem for the last time he is ready to declare himself to the whole world. He knows this will lead swiftly to his death, but it has always been God's plan. He prepares his disciples for what will happen. He will die in the place of others, like the Passover lamb. His blood will turn God's anger aside as he becomes the ultimate guilt offering. As he dies, the way to God's presence is opened up and Gentiles believe in him. Jesus is now the way to God, the only entry point

to God's Kingdom. Now all nations can have access to God, but only by becoming disciples of Jesus.

Significant Events   Ask the group to make a list of events they consider significant and list them on a board. Events can be personal, birthdays, house moves, new schools, etc., as well as national or international: a new head of state, sporting success, landing on the moon, etc. Discuss what makes events significant. In today's Bible study we will look at some of the most significant events for Christians.

1. Focus activity.

2. See what has been remembered about who Jesus is and what he has come to do. Present them in the same ways as we have done in the last 2 lessons. This will help your group to remember.

3. See what your group can remember about the order of events from Jesus' entry into Jerusalem to his ascension. Do this by providing strips of paper containing each event and asking the group to place them in the correct order.

4. Pick out the first one, 'The Entry into Jerusalem', to read and study briefly.

5. Pick out 'The Last Supper' and briefly summarise the events from Jesus' entry into Jerusalem. Point out that, through this familiar meal, Jesus was preparing his disciples for his death in a very memorable way. Briefly read and study the passage, drawing particular attention to the OT images Jesus is using.

6. Pick out 'The Death of Jesus', again briefly summarising the previous events. Read Psalm 22:1-18. If possible leave Psalm 22 open and, with another Bible, look up the account of the death of Jesus. Read and study this passage, referring to Psalm 22 where appropriate. Make sure that they understand that this Psalm was written around 1000 years before the death of Jesus.

7. Draw a new diagram to illustrate that access to God now comes through the death of Jesus. There is no other way.

8. Pick out 'The Ascension and the Great Commission'. Make sure that they understand the link between Jesus being the only way to God and the need to make disciples of all nations. Discuss what this means for us. Can people of other faiths come into God's Kingdom?

PREPARATION

Acts 1:1-11; 2:1-41; 7:54 - 8:8; 9:1 - 10:48; 13:4 - 18:23

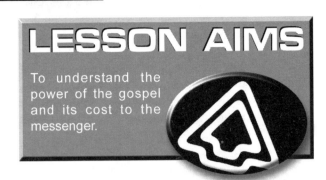

LESSON AIMS

To understand the power of the gospel and its cost to the messenger.

Our last study finished with Jesus' command to go and make disciples of all nations (Matthew 28:19). Throughout the Old Testament God made himself known to the world by his relationship with one nation, located in one geographical area. This instruction is quite different. God's people are being sent out to other nations. Now people will encounter God through the gospel message as it is brought to them by the apostles and others. Paul describes his job as carrying around in his body the death of Christ (2 Corinthians 4:10). People come face to face with Jesus through Paul and the apostolic message. No longer do the nations come to Israel, now Jesus goes to the world through his witnesses.

This would be a huge responsibility and would take great courage, but when God calls someone to a big task, he equips them to do it. In this study we see God equipping the believers and sending them out. Also we see God powerfully at work through the proclamation of the gospel and many becoming disciples of Jesus Christ.

1:3	Jesus starts to equip his apostles. To start with they need proof of his bodily resurrection and to understand the significance of what has happened.
1:4-5	But they need something else too. They need to be baptised with the Holy Spirit. As we mentioned earlier, this is a New Covenant phenomenon. Ordinary people did not receive the Holy Spirit in Old Testament times. But these are now the 'last days' when God pours out his Spirit on all people and everyone who calls on the name of the Lord will be saved (Joel 2:28,32 quoted in Acts 2:17-21). The Holy Spirit will equip them for the work Jesus is giving them to do. They are to stay in Jerusalem until this happens.
1:6	Still there is confusion about what Jesus has come to do. His disciples are still thinking that Jesus is going to be a recognisable king and restore a geographical kingdom.

1:7-8	Jesus redirects their thinking about the kingdom onto the given task. God's presence, through the Holy Spirit, will go out from Jerusalem to the whole world through their witness. The nations will not be drawn to a geographical Jerusalem with its temple, but will be drawn to Jesus as they encounter him through the apostles' message and become part of the Kingdom of God. This kingdom will consist of God's people, living under the authority of Jesus in their own land. They will enter the land that God has promised for his people only after death. Hebrews 11:10 tells us even Abraham knew this!
1:11	This is the way Jesus will return on the last day, as an adult man, in glory.

Acts 1:3-11 tells us that three things will happen:

1. The Holy Spirit will come upon them and they will receive power.

2. They will be witnesses to Jesus in Jerusalem, in Judea and Samaria and in all the earth.

3. Jesus will return in the same way they saw him depart.

The Coming of the Holy Spirit (Acts 2:1-13)

2:1	The day of Pentecost was a Jewish festival, celebrated 50 days after the Passover. What happened on this day of Pentecost was a miraculous, one off event.
2:2	The coming of the Holy Spirit on this occasion was visible. The wind noise and fire remind us of Mount Sinai and the awesome presence of God.
2:4	This does not seem to be the same as the gift of 'tongues'. They were speaking recognisable languages.
2:5	All the people gathered were Jews, in Jerusalem to participate in the festival. They had come from all over the place, so would have spoken different languages.

2:6	Everyone heard the message in their own language, no interpretation was needed. This was an authoritative message for all Israel, just like the events of Mount Sinai.
2:7	Everyone was amazed - what was happening was totally inexplicable.
2:12	They were also curious.

Witness in Jerusalem (Acts 2:14-41)

| 2:16 | These strange events are the fulfilment of Joel's prophecy. Peter is an ordinary man, yet he is prophesying. It is a sign that the new age, spoken of by Joel and the other prophets, has come. |
| 2:17-39 | Peter's message to the crowd consists of 4 main elements. (Subsequent addresses in Acts follow a similar pattern.)

1. A recounting of the ministry and death of Jesus.

2. Jesus' resurrection is God's endorsement of his claim to be Messiah and an indictment on them for rejecting him.

3. The use of the OT, particularly the words of David, to demonstrate that Jesus is the Messiah.

4. A call to repent and believe that Jesus is the Christ. |
| 2:41 | Through this proclamation of the gospel, large numbers of people become believers and are baptised. The church in Jerusalem starts to grow. |

Growth through difficulty

There continues to be growth (2:47; 5:14), despite opposition from the Jewish leaders (5:17-18,40; 6:8-11). Often these two seem to go hand in hand (4:1-4).

Authority demonstrated in miracle-working

The apostles perform miracles in Jesus' name. By this God shows that the apostles' words about Jesus are authoritative and from God (3:6-8; 5:12).

Taking up the cross

| 7:54-60 | Eventually there is martyrdom. Stephen follows the path to death like his Lord. There are many similarities in the account of Stephen's death and the account of the death of Jesus. We are meant to make the connection. |

Witness in Judea and Samaria

| 8:1 | God used the persecution which followed Stephen's death to take the gospel to Judea and Samaria. When one group of people reject Jesus, his message is taken to others. |
| 8:4-8 | The scattered disciples preach wherever they go. They seem to have understood that this message is for everyone. The Samaritans respond to the message of Jesus. |

The Gospel is for Gentiles as well as Jews

The apostles seem to need special reassurance that Gentiles can not only become believers, but 'brothers' (Ephesians 3:6).

In Acts 10 Peter learns at the house of Cornelius that, under the New Covenant, the old laws of Leviticus have been superseded. Gentiles do not have to become Jewish in order to be acceptable to God, but are equal heirs of the New Covenant promises. This seems very straightforward to us, but would have been very difficult for Jews like Peter to grasp.

In Acts 9 God calls a very special man to do a special job. Saul becomes God's apostle to the Gentiles (9:15).

Witness to the ends of the earth

11:19-21	The Good News reaches Antioch.
13:1-3	The church at Antioch send Paul and Barnabas on their first missionary journey (13:4 - 14:28).
15:36-18:22	Paul's second missionary journey.
16:6-10	Through a vision God directs Paul to take the gospel to Europe.
16:14	Lydia becomes the first European believer.
18:22	They arrive home at Antioch.
18:23	Paul sets out on his third missionary journey to visit some of the churches he has established in Galatia and Phrygia, then he moves on to Ephesus and Corinth.

When Paul arrived in a new place, he went to the synagogue first to tell the Jews their Messiah had come. Some believed, but generally Paul's message was rejected by the Jews and most vehemently by their leaders. So Paul took his message to the Gentiles and established churches, consisting of both believing Jews and Gentiles, which were totally separate from the synagogues. Everywhere Paul went there was opposition and rejection by some, but others who believed the gospel and entered the Kingdom of God. Often Paul would have to make a rapid exit from a place where his message had upset people, but this did not deter him, he just took his message to the next place he came to and began again, e.g. in Berea (17:10-14).

Paul's life was very difficult and uncomfortable. 2 Corinthians 11:24-29 detail some of the stresses Paul faced, but these difficulties did not put him off being God's messenger to the Gentiles. He saw that the glory to come would be well worth any suffering he might have to face during his earthly life. In fact, sharing in Christ's sufferings leads on to sharing in his glory (Romans 8:17-18). There were always people who opposed or ridiculed Paul. Some of the fiercest opposition he encountered came from within the newly formed churches.

Some of the Roman Emperors persecuted Christians and many trod the path of martyrdom, like Stephen. Yet nothing could stop the spread of the gospel and the growth of the church. The book of Acts finishes with the arrival of Paul in Rome, at the very centre of the then civilised world. From Rome the message was taken to all corners of the Roman Empire. By AD 314 there was a church in Britain, which was organised enough to send 3 bishops to an international synod, and the Roman Emperor Constantine had become a Christian.

Lesson Summary

The church started from very small beginnings, 11 apostles on a hillside, saying good-bye to their master. But they were equipped by the Holy Spirit to take Jesus to the whole world through their message. They started teaching the Jews in Jerusalem, but opposition and persecution drove the message outwards to the surrounding countryside. Opposition from the Jewish leaders did not stop the gospel, rather it aided its spread. It did not stop the apostles and others in their fearless proclamation and it did not stop people becoming disciples of Jesus. The growth of the Kingdom of God is under God's control and cannot be stopped.

Spreading the Word   Divide the group into teams, who stand at one end of the room. On the command to start, the first runner in each team runs to the other end of the room and back, catches hold of the second runner's hand and repeats the exercise. Continue until the whole team has run the length of the room and back holding hands. The first team to complete the exercise wins. Comment on more and more people joining the team as the race progressed. How easy was it for the first runners as more people joined the chain? Today's Bible study is about the way the good news about Jesus spread to more and more people. Let's see how it happened and how easy it was for the people who took the message to others.

Lesson Plan

1. Focus activity.
2. Bring a world map to the lesson and get the group to find countries they have visited. Each time ask if there were any churches there? There may be some people who come from other countries, or people known to your group who have moved to places like Australia. Ask if they will be able to join a church there? Find Israel on the map. See if you can calculate how far the gospel has travelled.

3. Read Acts 1:3-11 and identify the 3 things that are promised. Write these down as headings. (We will consider the second coming of Jesus next session.) Make sure that they understand what the confusion expressed in v.6 is all about. Make sure that they understand what the Kingdom of God is in a NT context.

4. Read Acts 2:1-12. Point out the OT images of God's presence. Make sure that they understand what being filled with the Holy Spirit involves and how it will equip the believers for their task.

5. Write down the headings, 'Preaching', 'Growth', 'Opposition', 'Miracles' and 'Spread'. Give each group member one or two references to find. Read them out as a group and match them to a heading. Explain how these were hallmarks of the early church and how God used each of these things. Particularly draw attention to opposition being a sign that the authentic message was being preached, not a sign that the apostles were doing it wrong.

6. See what the group can remember about the conversion of Paul and the job God had called him to. Using the map (page 80), track his missionary journeys, using the NIV headings in Acts 13-18. Draw their attention to the opposition Paul faced, the beatings and ridicule he suffered and, in spite of that, the huge impact of his ministry (looking up verses where appropriate).

7. Discuss why people are hostile to the Gospel of Jesus. In what ways do the young people experience opposition to their faith or suffering? Have they had bad experiences when trying to share their faith? Reassure them that this is normal Christian experience. Talk through ways in which they can be involved in evangelism, making sure that they are clear about the power of the gospel, but being realistic about the bravery this takes.

PREPARATION
Revelation 20:11 - 22:6, Matthew 24:36-44

LESSON AIMS
To understand how finally everything will be restored.

We live in what the Bible calls the 'last days', the time between the resurrection of Jesus and his coming in glory. This is the gospel age, the age of making disciples of all nations, whilst the fallen earth and its fallen people stumble on, most continuing to ignore God, but some in active rebellion against him. This age has lasted for nearly 2000 years, but it will end. That day is already set (Acts 17:31 - God has set a day when he will judge the world with justice).

What will happen when Jesus returns?

The Lord Jesus will return, suddenly, loudly, visibly and unmistakably (Matthew 24:29-30).

He will come in the same way as he left (Acts 1:11).

He will come in the clouds and every eye will see him (Revelation 1:7).

We do not know when he will come, only the Father knows (Matthew 24:36).

We cannot predict when he will come (Matthew 24:44).

How should we live in the light of this?

We should be watchful, ready at all times (Matthew 24:42,44).

We should live godly lives while we wait (Titus 2:12-13).

Jesus will judge all nations

We will all stand before the throne of Jesus. He is the judge (Matthew 25:31, Revelation 20: 11).

Everyone will be judged according to what he has done (Revelation 20:12, 2 Corinthians 5:10).

Unbelievers will be judged. Everything they have done and said will be remembered and taken into account (Matthew 12:36). Nothing can be hidden (Romans 2:16).

Believers will be judged (Romans 14:10-12) and the faithful will be rewarded (Matthew 25:34,21).

But every believer will be saved because of what Jesus has done, not because of what they have done (1 Peter 3:18, Ephesians 2:8, Revelation 20:15).

Jesus will destroy all evil

Everything that is sinful, fallen and rebellious will be done away with and destroyed for good (Revelation 21:8). There will be nothing left to oppose the rule of Jesus (2 Peter 3:10-13).

Jesus will establish a new creation (Revelation 21-22)

21:1	This comes into being after the destruction of the old creation.
21:2	There are 2 images here: a heavenly city and a bride. The Bride of Christ is the church, so what is being described here is the community of believers, descending from heaven to the new earth.
21:3	Now God can live with men. He does not need a tabernacle anymore (21:22). There is unhindered relationship, just as there was in the Garden of Eden.
21:4	There will be no more suffering, because the fallen world and all its fallen relationships have passed away.
21:5	We are now back in the time of John. Jesus is telling John to write this down because he is sure to do it.
21:6-8	God will give this inheritance to his sons. Their future is secure, though the present may involve overcoming suffering and difficulty. The wicked will certainly be destroyed.
21:10-14	Now the Holy City is pictured as a structure, rather than a community.
21:15-21	Its splendour is beyond imagination.
21:22	There is no temple, because God can dwell with his people without the need for such things.
21:24	The people living in the city include Gentiles (the nations and kings of the earth). God promised that all people would be blessed through God's covenant with Abraham and here they are.
21:25	The gates never shut; access to God is never shut off. The barring of people from God's presence will never happen here, as it did in Eden.
21:27	There is no possibility of it being spoiled, like Eden. There is no possibility of any entering it who do not know Jesus.

22:1	This is reminiscent of the rivers flowing out from Eden.
22:2	The tree of life is accessible and for the nations. This is a reversal of the effects of the Fall, when access to the tree of life was denied to Adam and Eve.
22:3-4	God's servants will be able to come freely before the throne of God and see him face to face.

Lesson Summary

We are living in the last days, the time between the resurrection of Jesus and his coming again. We do not know when Jesus will come again, but we know that he will and that it will be glorious and unmistakable. He will judge all people and then destroy completely everything which is fallen and rebellious. There will be nothing left to oppose the rule of Jesus.

Then Jesus will establish a new creation, which will be like Eden, only better, and unable to be spoiled. In this new creation we will see the promises made to Abraham fulfilled in full. God's redeemed people, made perfect, will live in God's place, the new creation, under the authority of Jesus and in perfect fellowship with him. It is exactly what we were made for at the beginning of time and will be worth waiting for. It will be worth suffering for and will be more wonderful than we can ever imagine.

Being Ready Divide the group into teams of 4-5. Give each team a pile of newspapers, sellotape, string, a stapler and scissors. Explain that one of their number has been invited to an important party (or similar event) and the car has arrived to take them. Unfortunately, they are not ready. The teams have to fashion an appropriate outfit from the newspaper and dress up one of their number. At the end of a set period of time call a halt and judge the results. Comment on the need to be ready for an important occasion. Let's see what the Bible has to say about being ready for the most important occasion of our lives.

Lesson Plan

1. Focus activity.
2. Get the group to remember how things were in the Garden of Eden by recreating the Garden plan from Week 2. Remember what happened when Adam and Eve rebelled against God:

   ♦ Their relationship with God was spoiled.

   ♦ Their relationships with each other were spoiled.

♦ The world became spoiled and unable to be ruled over.

♦ People could no longer exercise dominion over the animals.

♦ The ground became difficult and frustrating to cultivate.

♦ Death came into the world.

♦ The people were cast out of God's presence.

You could do this using picture or word prompts. Put them into a hat or bag and ask group members to pick one out and try to remember what it refers to. Other group members can offer help.

3. Write in the middle of a large sheet of paper, 'The Second Coming of Jesus'. Divide into pairs and give them a selection of references to look up (1 or 2 each). Feed back to the group and write the answers radiating out from 'The Second Coming of Jesus' statement. Ask what we should do in the meantime? After they have come up with some suggestions, look at Matthew 24:42-44 and Titus 2:12-13.

4. Repeat this activity for 'The Judgment'. If we know that judgment is coming, how should that motivate us now? Be prepared for discussion. They may have lots of questions. If you are not too clear about possible answers, look at a systematic theology book prior to the lesson. (Suggested books are 'Know the Truth' by Bruce Milne and 'Systematic Theology' by Wayne Grudem, both published by IVP.)

5. Read Revelation 21:1 - 22:6. Write down 'The New Creation'. What will the new creation be like? Get the group to contribute answers. How is this description like Eden? How is it better than Eden?

6. Discuss what things about this life they dislike. How will these things differ in the new creation? (Some of these are likely to be due to their sinful nature, rather than to the fallen world. It would be a good opportunity to point out that they will be renewed and made perfect on that day, as well as everything around them.)

7. Complete the Bible timeline. (Timeline Pages 81-87)

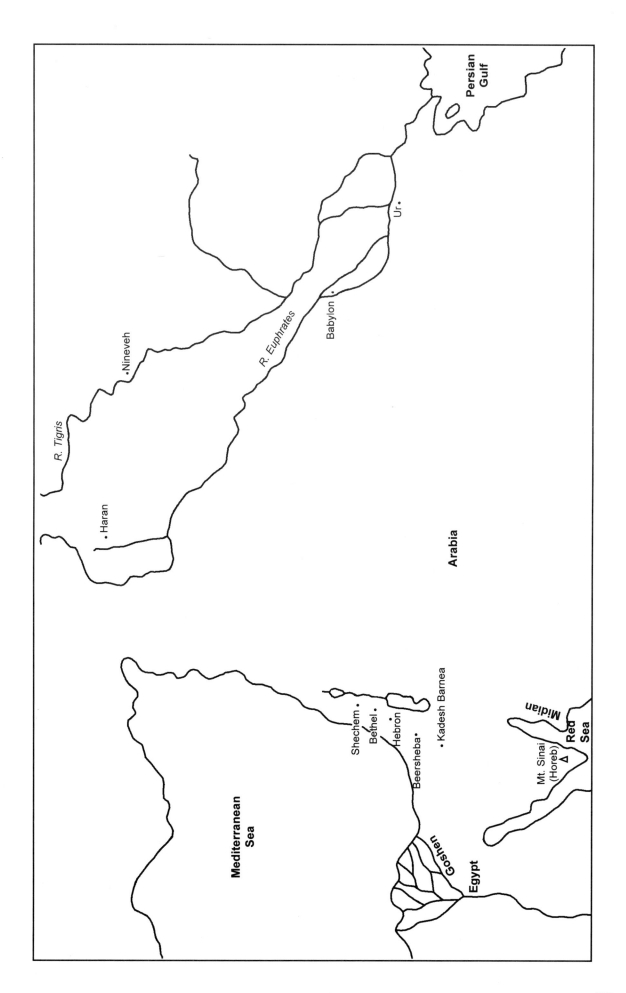

Persian
Gulf

R. Tigris

.Nineveh

R. Euphrates

Babylon .

Ur .

. Haran

Arabia

Mediterranean
Sea

Shechem .
Bethel .
Hebron .
Beersheba .

. Kadesh Barnea

Goshen

Egypt

Midian

Mt. Sinai
(Horeb)
△

Red
Sea

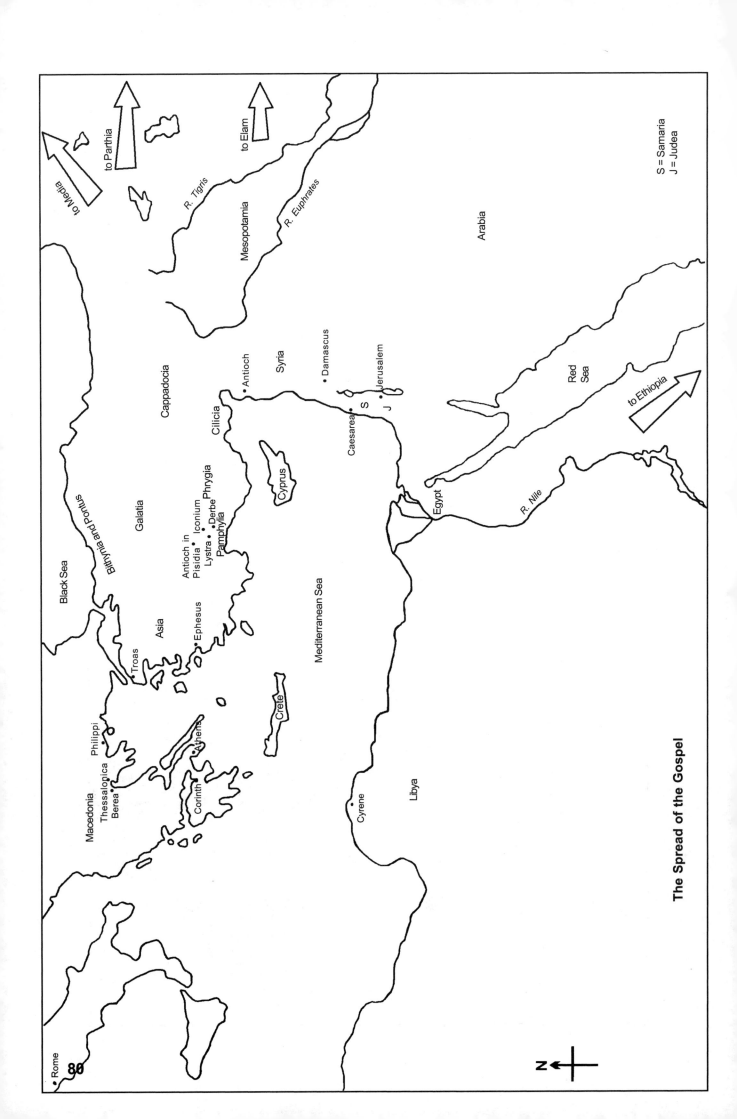

The Spread of the Gospel

S = Samaria
J = Judea

to Media

to Parthia

to Elam

to Ethiopia

R. Tigris

R. Euphrates

Mesopotamia

Arabia

Red Sea

R. Nile

Egypt

Syria

Damascus

Antioch

Jerusalem

Caesarea

S

J

Cappadocia

Cilicia

Cyprus

Crete

Phrygia

Derbe

Lystra

Iconium

Antioch in Pisidia

Pamphylia

Galatia

Bithynia and Pontus

Asia

Ephesus

Troas

Black Sea

Mediterranean Sea

Libya

Cyrene

Macedonia

Philippi

Thessalonica

Berea

Corinth

Athens

Rome

N

80

Bible Timeline

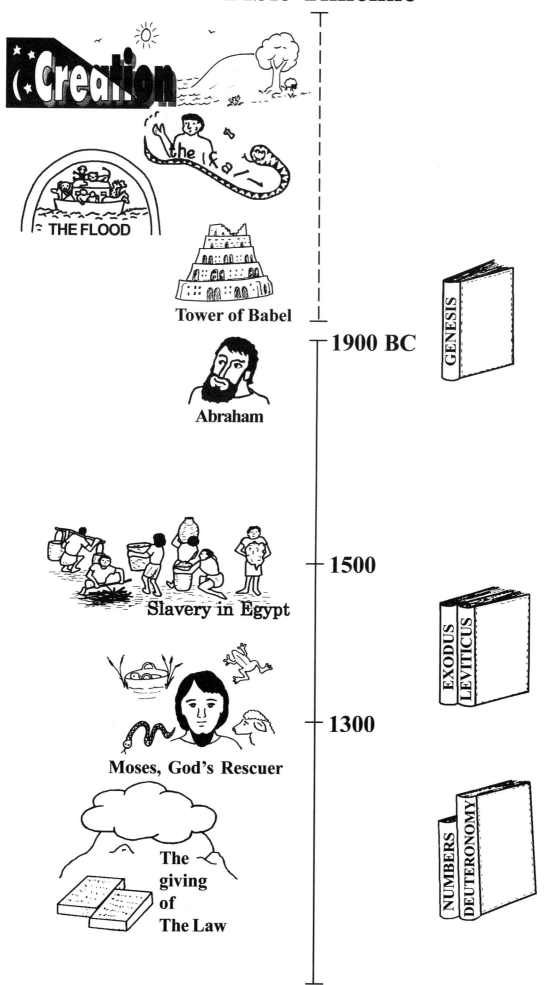

Creation

THE FLOOD

Tower of Babel

— 1900 BC

Abraham

GENESIS

Slavery in Egypt

— 1500

Moses, God's Rescuer

— 1300

EXODUS LEVITICUS

The giving of The Law

NUMBERS DEUTERONOMY

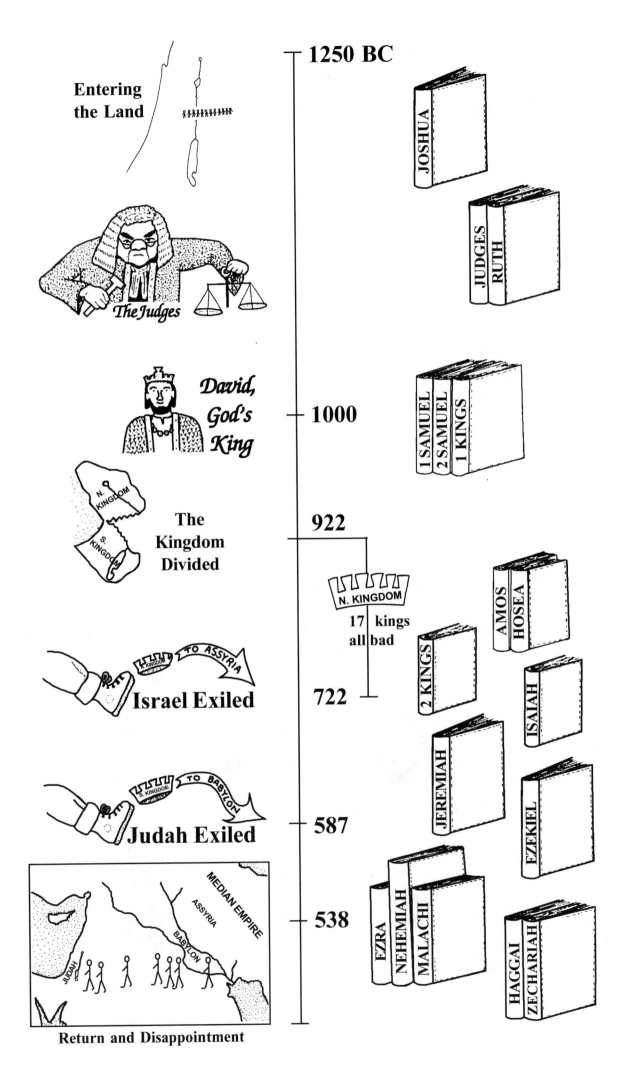

1250 BC

Entering the Land

JOSHUA

The Judges

JUDGES RUTH

David, God's King

1000

1 SAMUEL 2 SAMUEL 1 KINGS

The Kingdom Divided

922

N. KINGDOM

17 kings all bad

AMOS HOSEA

Israel Exiled

722

2 KINGS

ISAIAH

Judah Exiled

587

JEREMIAH

EZEKIEL

538

EZRA NEHEMIAH MALACHI

HAGGAI ZECHARIAH

Return and Disappointment

82

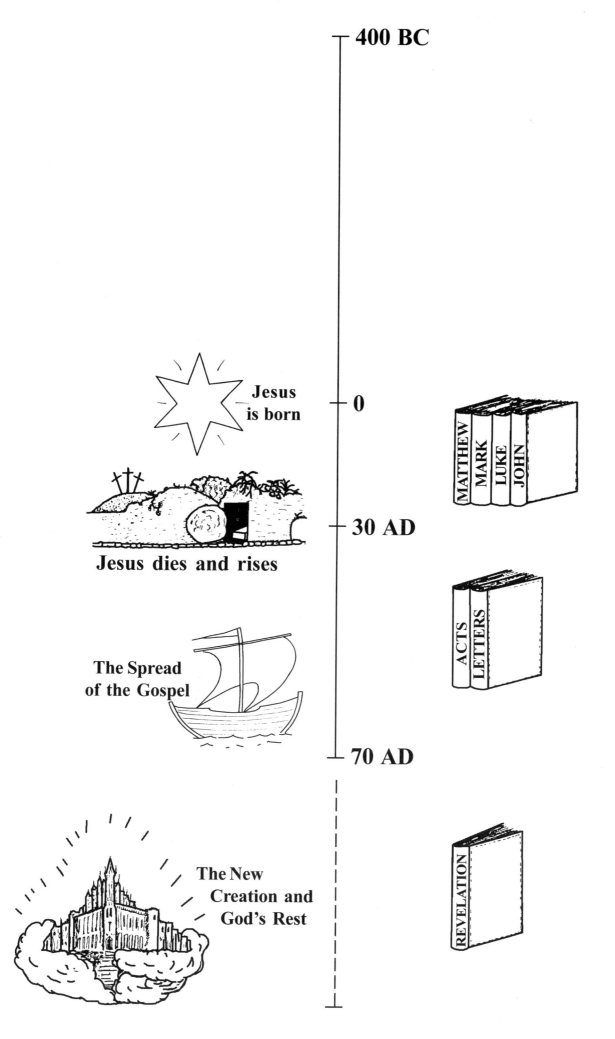

400 BC

Jesus
is born

0

MATTHEW MARK LUKE JOHN

Jesus dies and rises

30 AD

The Spread
of the Gospel

ACTS LETTERS

70 AD

The New
Creation and
God's Rest

REVELATION

Bible Timeline Activity

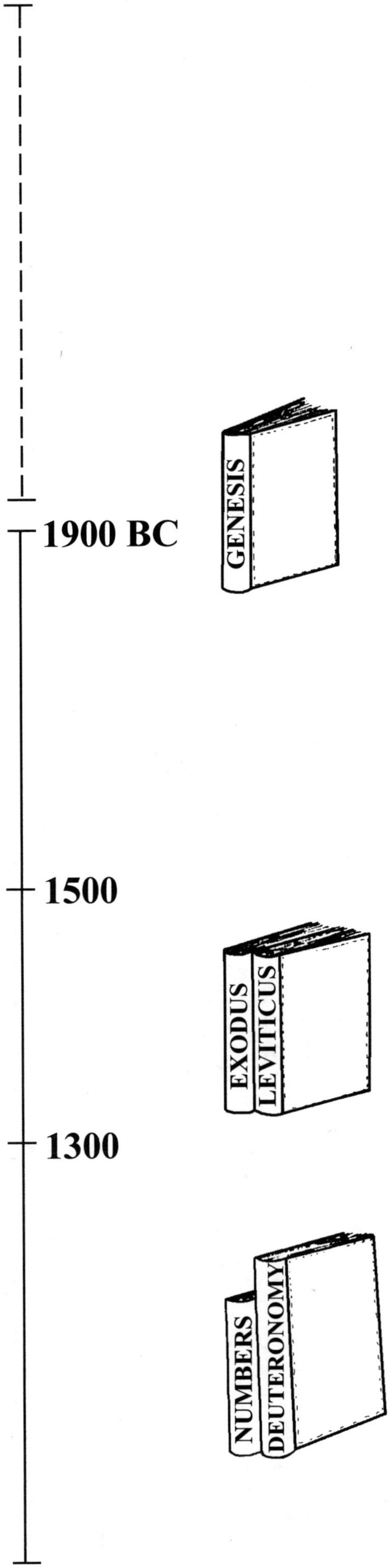

1900 BC

GENESIS

1500

EXODUS LEVITICUS

1300

NUMBERS DEUTERONOMY

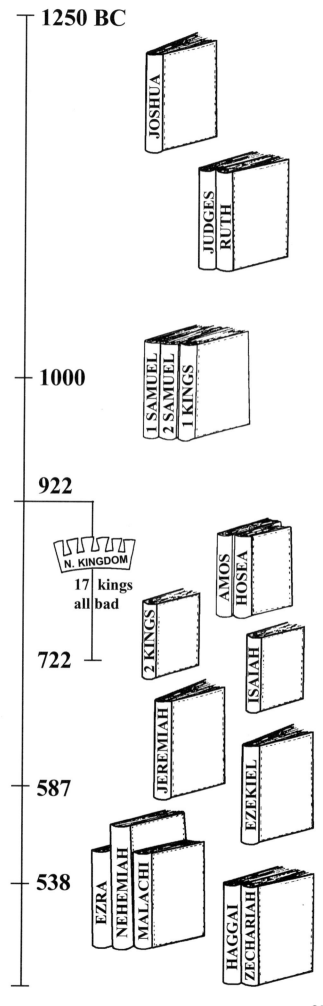

1250 BC

JOSHUA

JUDGES
RUTH

1000

1 SAMUEL
2 SAMUEL
1 KINGS

922

N. KINGDOM

17 kings
all bad

2 KINGS

AMOS
HOSEA

722

ISAIAH

JEREMIAH

587

EZEKIEL

EZRA
NEHEMIAH
MALACHI

538

HAGGAI
ZECHARIAH

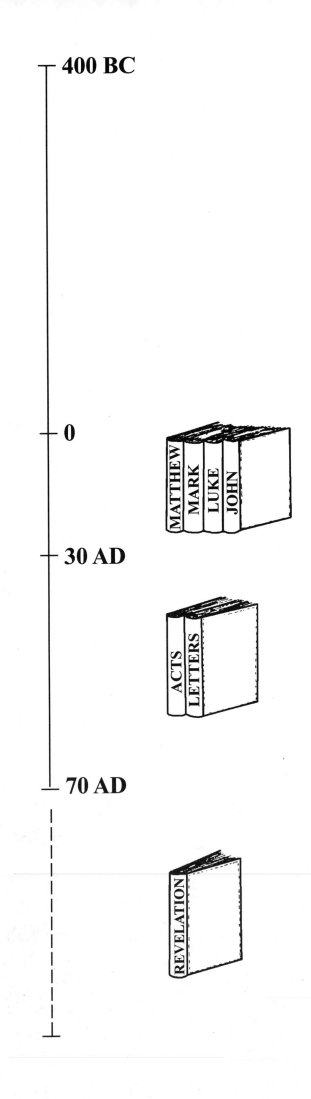

400 BC

0

MATTHEW MARK LUKE JOHN

30 AD

ACTS LETTERS

70 AD

REVELATION

Jesus is born

Entering the Land

Israel Exiled

Judah Exiled

The New Creation and God's Rest

Jesus dies and rises

The Kingdom Divided

The Judges

The Spread of the Gospel

The giving of The Law

Moses, God's Rescuer

THE FLOOD

David, God's King

Tower of Babel

Return and Disappointment

Abraham

Creation

Slavery in Egypt

Joseph's Family Tree

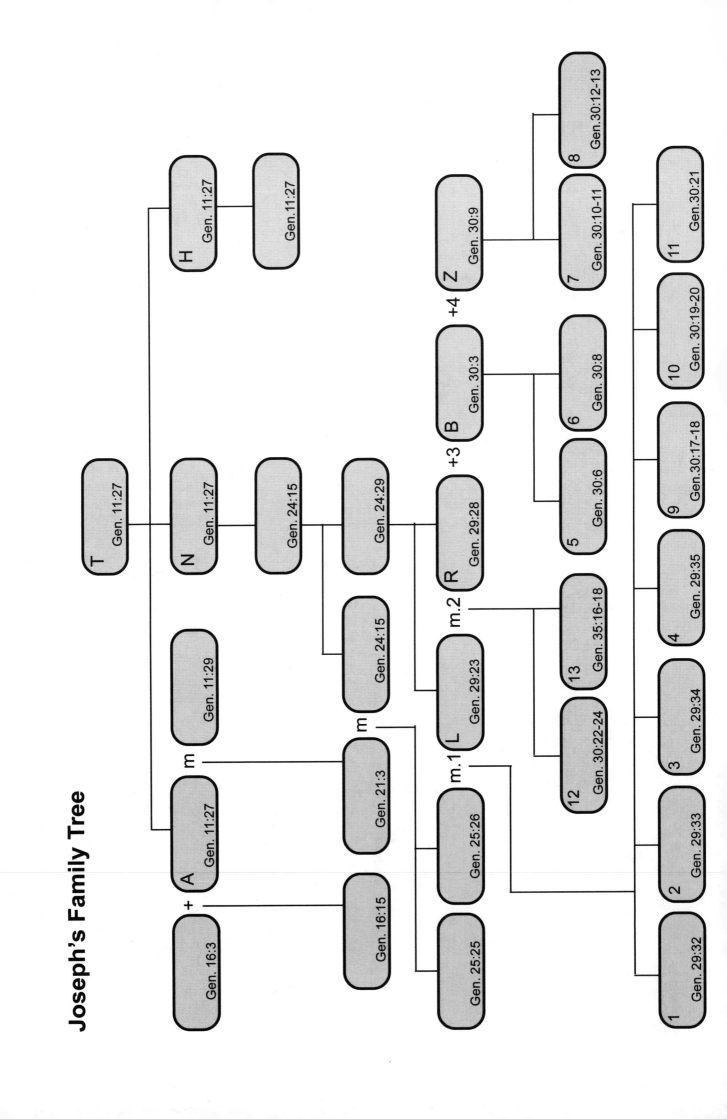

Anointing of David
(God looks on the heart)

harp

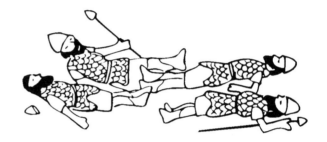

Victory over the Philistines

Jonathan recognises David's anointing

Saul tries to kill David

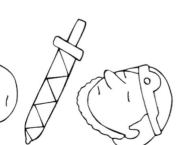

Saul and Jonathan die in battle

David becomes king

David and Goliath

Notes

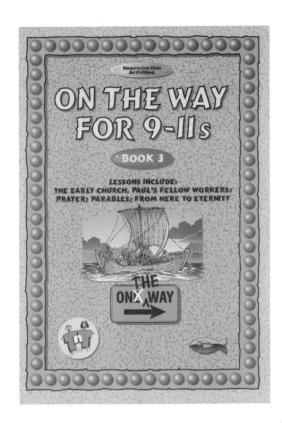

The On the Way series can cater for all your teaching needs.

* Preschool - Three books - Beginning witht he Bible First Class; Beginning with the Bible - Old Testament - Beginning with the Bible New Testament.

* 3-9's - Fourteen books covering all the major doctrines of the Christian Faith.

* 9-11's - Six books giving children a solid introduction to Bible Study.

* 11-14's - Six books to challenge and stretch young teens;

building on the 9-11s series.

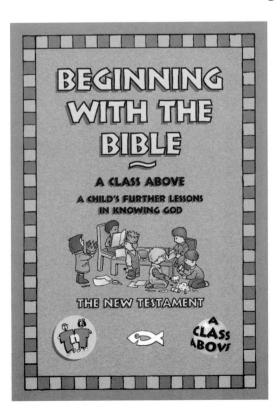

The Game is up

A series of four games books that cover the old and new testaments. These books not only give a wide selection of games for a variety of situations but they are also flexible enough to be used with any sunday school or kids club curriculum. Why not add another dimension to your teaching programme. These are not just games books - they are so much more!

Other Resources available from
Christian Focus Publications

If you want to get your children's group involved in mission: then this is the book for you. With activity sheets and photocopiable resources this book introduces personal and world wide mision in a fun and effective way. ISBN: 1857924460

How about finding out who Jesus really is? You can tell a lot about him by looking that all the names he has! Photocopiable resources throughout make this a workbook you will use time and time again. ISBN: 1857926501

This resource book is excellent for children's groups and families alike - an excellent devotional way into the life and theology of the Lord Jesus Christ. ISBN:1857925599

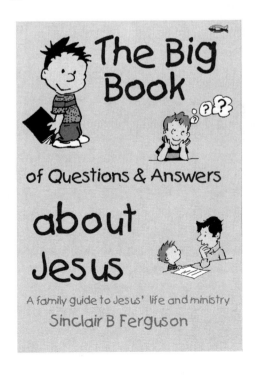

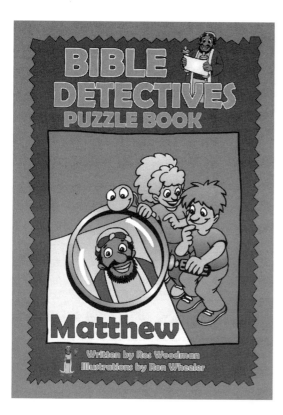

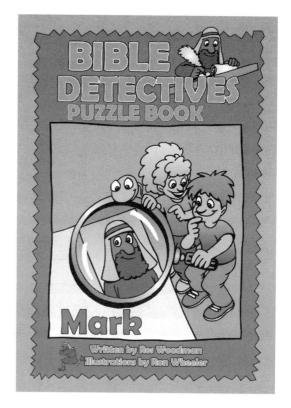

Join the
Bible Detectives

as they puzzle their way through the gospels with these fun and interactive work books. Matthew, Mark, Luke and John all tell us about Jesus in their own unique ways -
ISBN: 1857926730; 1857926749; 1857927583; 1857927591

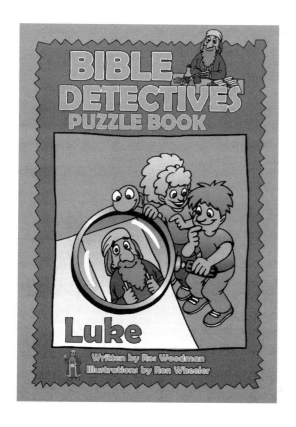

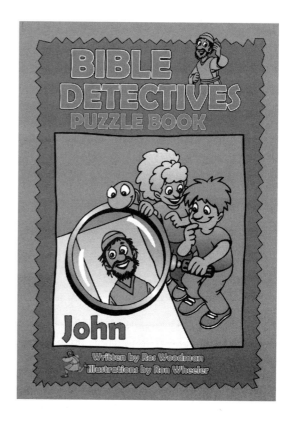

Syllabus for On The Way for 11-14s

Book 1 (28 weeks)		Book 3 (28 weeks)		Book 5 (26 weeks)	
Abraham	(7)	Joseph	(7)	Bible Overview	(26)
Jacob	(7)	People in Prayer	(7)		
The Messiah (Christmas)	(2)	The Saviour of the World (Christmas)	(3)		
Jesus said, 'I am …'	(7)	Is God Fair? (Predestination)	(2)		
Ruth	(5)	Learning from a Sermon	(3)		
		The Sermon on the Mount	(6)		

Book 2 (25 weeks)		Book 4 (25 weeks)		Book 6 (27 weeks)	
Rescue (Easter)	(3)	Psalms (Easter)	(2)	A Selection of Psalms	(5)
Paul (Acts 9-16)	(7)	Paul's Latter Ministry	(7)	The Normal Christian Life	(7)
Philippians	(5)	Colossians	(5)	Revelation	(9)
Paul (Acts 17-18)	(3)	Choose Life (Hell & Judgment)	(2)	Homosexuality	(1)
1 Thessalonians	(6)	The Kings	(9)	The Dark Days of the Judges	(5)
Suffering	(1)				

The books can be used in any order.

The number in brackets indicates the number of lessons in a series.

For more information about *On the Way for 11-14s* please contact:
Christian Focus Publications, Fearn, Tain, Ross-shire, IV20 1TW / Tel: +44 (0) 1862 871 011 or
TnT Ministries, 29 Buxton Gardens, Acton, London, W3 9LE / Tel: +44 (0) 20 8992 0450

CHRISTIAN FOCUS
Good books with the real message of hope!

Christian Focus Publications publishes biblically-accurate books for adults and children. If you are looking for quality Bible teaching for children then we have a wide and excellent range of Bible story books - from board books to teenage fiction, we have it covered. You can also try our new Bible teaching Syllabus for 3-9 year olds and teaching materials for pre-school children. These children's books are bright, fun and full of biblical truth, an ideal way to help children discover Jesus Christ for themselves. Our aim is to help children find out about God and get them enthusiastic about reading the Bible, now and later in their lives. Find us at our web page: www.christianfocus.com

TnT Ministries

TnT Ministries (which stands for Teaching and Training Ministries) was launched in February 1993 by Christians from a broad variety of denominational backgrounds who were concerned that teaching the Bible to children be taken seriously. The leaders were in charge of the Sunday School of 50 teachers at St Helen's Bishopsgate, an evangelical church in the City of London, for 13 years, during which time a range of Biblical teaching materials was developed. TnT Ministries also runs training days for Sunday School teachers.

ON THE WAY

BOOK 5 for 11-14 Yr Olds

Do you want to encourage young people to read the Bible? Do you want young people to realise that the Bible is God's guide for them, relevant, exciting, dynami TnT Ministries have developed 'On The Way' to meet your needs, the needs of your church and most importantly the needs of the young people you teach.

You will be On the Way with these seven steps to success.

Reproducible
The activities are photocopiable so one book is all you need per teacher.

Interactive
Young people learn the skills to help them study God's word for themselves.

Comprehensive
A three year syllabus covers all the major doctrines of the Christian faith.

Enjoyable
Young people will love it and learn from it - so you will love teaching it too.

Biblical
Students and teachers learn together as everyone gets into the Bible.

Teacher friendly
Lesson plans and preparation tips make this series one you will recommend to others. It's designed by teachers who teach teachers!

Trustworthy
Edited by David Jackman of the Proclamation Trust this material has been tested in a variety of different denominational settings. It's worthwhile and it works.

Churches around the world from America to France, Spai to Korea, Hong Kong to Australia have discovered the strength of this Sunday school syllabus.
It is biblical, undated, multi-age, chronological and informative. Leaders and students are learning together the world over with the On The Way series - a unique and excellent curriculum.

TAKE NOTE: The On The Way Series can cater for all your teaching needs.

● **Pre-school** - Three books - Beginning with the Bible First Class; Beginning with the Bible - Old Testament; Beginning with the Bible - New Testament.

● **3-9s** - Fourteen books covering all the major doctrines of the Christian faith.

● **9-11s** - Six books giving children a solid introduction to Bible Study.

● **11-14s** - Six books to challenge and stretch young teens; building on the 9-11's series.

Challenging and intellectually stimulating this is the obvious 'next stage' for the 11-14 year old class. With less focus on craft there is more focus on hard hitting issues with group discussion times. An excellent resource to help young people think for themselves in a Biblical way.

● **The Game is Up** - A selection of Games books to add another dimension to your teaching programme. Not just a games book - it's so much more.

● **Teacher Training Video**
Over 5 hours of practical, interactive, training.

It doesn't matter if you are in a church, community hall or sports complex. On the Way i ough to suit a wide variety of situations.

It doesn't matter how many children you have. You can have six or twenty-six. You just p he activity pages - there are no extra magazines to buy.

It doesn't matter if your children come from a churched or un-churched background. The On The Way series teaches God's word simply and effectively.

J24 Sunday School Information
and Resources
YCK/CHD/EDU

ISBN 1-85792-708-7

9 781857 927085

The changing
ROLE AND STATUS OF WOMEN
during the 20th century

HOW DID EMPLOYMENT domestic OPPORTUNITIES FOR WOMEN ideology IN WALES AND ENGLAND Christabel Pankhurst CHANGE AFTER THE SECOND homemakers WORLD WAR? Irene Ward SINGLE PARENTHOOD Women fashion designers Women as Increased free time business bilateral schools the marriage bar leaders THE MEANS TEST HOW WERE WOMEN EMPLOYED IN THE EARLY TWENTIETH CENTURY IN WALES AND ENGLAND? positive discrimination Birth control ZANDRA RHODES THE IMPACT OF THE FIRST WORLD WAR THE FEMALE EUNUCH Ellen Wilkinson Megan Lloyd George Household and family tasks and routines 'Upstairs, Downstairs' Women's work after the war modern housecraft David Lloyd George

THE ABORTION ACT Women's work after the war Improved educational opportunities Harriet Harman Women in the 1930s Women in the munitions factories Changes in female representation in Westminster since 1985 Y Wawr Newsom Education Report 'Deeds, not words' Edith Summerskill Amenities and further improvements MARY QUANT WHAT WAS Gwyneth Dunwoody Aneurin Bevan BREAKING THROUGH THE 'GLASS CEILING' THE ROLE OF WOMEN IN representation of women in parliament THE HOME IN WALES SUFFRAGISTS AND AND ENGLAND IN SUFFRAGETTES the House of Commons THE EARLY TWENTIETH INCREASED summun CENTURY? maternal FREE Homes for Today mortality TIME and Tomorrow Caroline Lucas Barbara Castle Labour-saving devices The impact of women's magazines Work in light industry modern homes Women in education Opportunities in radio and television The Descent of Woman: The Classic Study of Evolution The impact of the Second World War Women's Auxiliary Air Force HOW SUCCESSFUL HAVE WOMEN Margaret Bondfield BEEN IN TAKING ADVANTAGE OF munitionettes NEW EMPLOYMENT OPPORTUNTIES IN WALES AND ENGLAND? Moves towards equality Changes in education J. K. Rowling Nurses, doctors and women police The Equal Opportunities Commission HAVE WOMEN BENEFITTED FROM UK GOVERNMENT LEGISLATION SINCE THE 1960s? The Representation of the People Act, 1918 Betty Boothroyd Millicent Garrett Fawcett Women's Land Army Mo Mowlam The success of female role models HOW HAVE CHANGES IN HOME AND FAMILY LIFE IN RECENT TIMES AFFECTED WOMEN IN WALES AND ENGLAND?

Household and family tasks and routines Laura Ashley Family planning Government legislation IMPROVEMENTS IN HOUSING HOW SUCCESSFUL HAVE WOMEN BEEN IN ACHIEVING IMPORTANT POLITICAL ROLES IN WALES AND ENGLAND? Ann Clwyd Emmeline Pankhurst The impact of increased opportunities in secondary and higher education Cosmopolitan Women's Land Army Larger post-war housing Domestic service preventative health measures Fitness and leisure advice Lady Nancy Astor The Sex Discrimination Act

The achievements of women in modern political life Emily Wilding Davison HOW DID LIFE FOR WOMEN AT HOME IN WALES AND ENGLAND CHANGE AFTER THE SECOND WORLD WAR? Changes in working opportunities The Women's Liberation Movement THE WELSH GOVERNMENT The traditional role of women Women in the Services Margaret Thatcher Spare Rib HOW MUCH SUCCESS DID WOMEN ACHIEVE IN THE FIGHT FOR POLITICAL RIGHTS IN WALES AND ENGLAND IN THE EARLY TWENTIETH CENTURY? Women's Lib Germaine Greer Women's Hour Votes for women Traditional employment The formation of the National Assembly for Wales Family planning and patterns Anita Roddick Eleanor Rathbone Revival of feminism in the late 1960s and early 1970s

PRIFYSGOL ABERYSTWYTH

Colin P. F. Hughes,
Catrin Stevens
and R. Paul Evans